Have you ever longed for a wise guide to turn to when you need help, to show you the right way to look at things? With *There Is No Somewhere Else* Francis Pring-Mill becomes that guide, giving you ancient, yet timeless wisdom on how to be in natural harmony with life. Don't miss this opportunity to learn how to use these universal principles in all aspects of your life. This is one of those books to keep on your nightstand because it will help you over and over again!

– Jean Haner, author of *The Five-Element Solution: Discover the Spiritual Side of Chinese Medicine*

There is No Somewhere Else grows on you as you allow the journey of the book to unfold. And by the end you may find the meaning in the title really striking. Drawing effectively from Stephen Mitchell's translation of the *Tao Te Ching*, Francis Pring-Mill offers a bracingly nourishing unpacking of "the Tao" and how living in accord with "the way things are" can look and feel. While there are many translations of the *Tao Te Ching*—a small book of 81 short verses—it's rare to find a refreshingly unadorned exploration and in-depth reflection on just what "Taoist wisdom" is like when lived.

Dr. Pring-Mill's colleague-like conversational tone makes these profound philosophical explorations rather fun. It's also refreshing to find a new book which "translates" these ancient Taoist insights into bite-sized (but not watered down) reflections readily available for the minds of today. But beware! *There is No Somewhere Else* will stop you in your tracks—if you let it—and the views from this mountain top, as Lao Tzu pointed out, will guide you.

– Kolin Lymworth, Founder of Banyen Books, Vancouver, BC

Praise for There is No Somewhere Else

Francis Pring-Mill is an experienced traveler who can lead us to the ancient Tao. While the Way might be steep, he is a worthy and generous guide. Grounded firmly in the ideas of the *Tao Te Ching*, *There Is No Somewhere Else* will reward frequent readings with many profound insights.

– Deng Ming-Dao, author of *365 Tao*, *The Lunar Tao* and *Chronicles of Tao*

The *Tao Te Ching* tells us that the Tao cannot be named, but that doesn't mean that a window can't be opened for us to see it whirling, creating, and transforming the world around us. Francis Pring-Mill's *There is No Somewhere Else* is just such a window that makes the esoteric lessons of Taoism clearer and illuminates the Tao's energies at work. Even more, this book provides valuable insights and reflections to recognize the currents of the Tao flowing in life by lighting a passageway toward deeper wisdom and peace.

– David Clippinger, Ph.D., author of *Cultivating Qi*, Director of Still Mountain T'ai Chi and Chi Kung, Executive Director of One Pine Institute

Francis Pring-Mill's *There is No Somewhere Else* takes us on an inspired journey through the timeless wisdom of the *Tao Te Ching*. With its meditative reflections and breathtaking nature photos, this beautiful book encourages us to see beyond distractions, embrace the present moment, and realize our oneness with the flow of life.

– Diane Dreher, Ph.D., author of *The Tao of Inner Peace*

Francis takes the profound texts from the *Tao Te Ching* and assembles a timeless piece of both poetry and prose with a clear and understandable application to everyday living. He reminds us to let the universe unfold through our own actions by being present in the moment. Francis provides comfort while guiding us toward a more peaceful and enlightened existence. His Taoist humanitarian wisdom presents a simple and beautiful approach to life that can heal ourselves and the world around us, "Aim to create harmony. Forget desire and expectation. Act with intent and caring. Then let go."

– Michael A. Allen, M.Phil., author of Pulitzer Prize nominated *Tao of Surfing: Finding Depth at Low Tide* and Producer/Co-Screenwriter for the award-winning feature film *A Long Road to Tao*

It is a delight to find this insightful and creative way of interpreting Tao wisdom from Dr. Pring-Mill's new book *There is No Somewhere Else*. It is clear from reading his work, he has found a well-balanced East/West synthesis within. He shares with us his personal learning, awareness and insight along the way—probing, searching with honesty and simple ease, entertaining his readers with seemingly unanswerable questions.

I am reminded of my learning from several of my mentors, kindred spirit soul mates such as Alan W. Watts with his belief in "the eternal now," Ram Dass's "Be Here Now," and Joseph Campbell's "follow your bliss." As well as recalling T.S. Eliot's lines "to arrive where we started and know the place for the first time." Pring-Mill reminds us, "Only the present moment is home. Everything else is somewhere else. Come home."

Again, what I appreciate in this new book is the simple ease of wisdom we can incorporate into our "moment to moment" life's journey. As an octogenarian approaching another decade ahead myself, I would attempt to declare with ease and joy, borrowing the title of this book, "There Is No Somewhere Else" and happily coming home to be here in the Tao, simply being alive with much gratitude.

– Chungliang Al Huang, author of *Embrace Tiger, Return to Mountain* and *Essential Tai Ji*, co-author with Alan W. Watts of *Tao: The Watercourse Way*, co-author with Jerry Lynch of *Thinking Body, Dancing Mind* and *Tao Mentoring*, Founder-director of Living Tao Foundation / Lan Ting Institute

In *There Is No Somewhere Else: Insights from the Tao Te Ching*, Francis Pring-Mill weaves together new poetic insight with stimulating questions about the nature of reality, and offers a fresh interpretation of the timeless wisdom of Lao Tsu's *Tao Te Ching*. Dr. Pring-Mill's analysis is clear and thoughtful, even as he points to powerful experiences that transcend the limitations of thought. The stunning black-and-white photographs are an essential part of the book, silently providing a view of the beauty and spaciousness of the wordless, eternal Tao. This is a guidebook for living—an invitation to the deep reflection that will lead each reader to experience the Oneness and Wholeness that is ever-present, the essence of the Tao.

– Linda Holiday, author of *Journey to the Heart of Aikido: The Teachings of Motomichi Anno Sensei*

There Is No Somewhere Else

Also by Francis Pring-Mill

In Harmony with the Tao: A Guided Journey into the Tao Te Ching

There Is No Somewhere Else

Insights from the Tao Te Ching

Francis Pring-Mill

All rights reserved. Copyright © 2024 by Francis Pring-Mill. No part of this book may be reproduced or transmitted in any form or by any means whatsoever, including graphic, electronic, or mechanical, including photocopying, recording, taping, or by any information storage or retrieval system, without permission from the publisher.

All text from Tao Te Ching by Lao Tzu, A New English Version, with Foreword and Notes, by Stephen Mitchell. Translation copyright © 1988 by Stephen Mitchell.

Published by

www.francispringmill.com

Interior images by Francis Pring-Mill
Cover and interior design by Christy Day, Constellation Book Services

ISBN (paperback): 978-1-7387668-4-0
ISBN (ebook): 978-1-7387668-5-7
ISBN (hardcover): 978-1-7387668-6-4

Printed in the United States of America

Contents

Preface	xiii
PART 1: A JOURNEY	xix
1: WHY YOU ARE HERE	1
2: CENTER YOURSELF IN THE TAO	7
3: LIFE IS RELATIONSHIP	13
4: WATCH YOUR THOUGHTS	17
5: JUST BE	21
6: LET THE LIGHT SHINE	25
7: LIVING IN AWARENESS	29
8: LET GO	33
9: TO SEE LIGHT	37
10: LISTEN FOR THE HARMONY	41
11: POINT OF VIEW	45
12: FREEDOM FROM DESIRE	51
13: MUSIC	57
14: THOUGHTS AND DREAMS	61
15: ON THE OTHER SIDE	67
16: INSIDE THE BOX	71
17: TEACHERS AND FRIENDS	77
18: TURN OFF THE FLASHLIGHT	81
19: INTENTION	87
20: EXPERIENCE AND REALITY	91
21: TRUE ARTISTS	97
22: REVEALING THE PATTERN	101
23: BE LIKE WATER	105
24: THE WHOLE TRUTH	109
25: LET YOURSELF GO	113

26: WE ARE HERE TO AWAKEN	119
27: INSIDE THE DREAM	125
28: FOCUS ON THE STEPS	131
29: JUST FOR TODAY	137
30: NOW IS ALL THERE IS	141
31: IN THE MOMENT	145
32: WHAT IF	149
33: THIS WORLD	153
34: INSIDE EVERY MOMENT	159
35: YOU ARE NOT ALONE	163
36: NO OTHER WAY	167
37: THERE IS NO SOMEWHERE ELSE	171
38: EACH OF US IS THE UNIVERSE	175
PART 2: A MAP	181

Only the present moment is home.
Everything else is somewhere else.
Come home.

Preface

From time to time, we have all likely asked ourselves the question, Is there a way to live our lives in harmony with the world around us? The *Tao Te Ching* says yes. That answer has inspired the collection of observations in this book.

The *Tao Te Ching* is a Chinese text written over twenty-five hundred years ago by a man named Lao Tzu. It consists of 81 brief chapters and has been a source of inspiration for centuries. You have likely heard quotes from it even if you didn't know where they came from. For example, "The journey of a thousand miles begins with a single step" (chapter 64).

I have been fascinated by this text ever since being a teenager and coming across a copy in a secondhand bookstore. I found I kept returning to it on and off over the years, and I always promised myself that one day I would take the time to explore why the text resonated so deeply with me. A few years ago I did that, and my book *In Harmony with the Tao: A Guided Journey into the Tao Te Ching* was the result. This book is written in the same spirit.

The *Tao Te Ching* is about the Tao, which is the great Oneness/Wholeness that encompasses everything. It is infinite and timeless. And we are part of it, although we spend much of our time imagining we are separate and alone. The Tao is also continuously unfolding, regardless of what we do. And we have a choice. We can either live in harmony with it or stand separate and apart and attempt to impose our will. Every day we have countless opportunities to make this choice and, consciously or unconsciously, we make choices all the time. But the consequences are profound. This is what the *Tao Te Ching* explores; and it does so in a special way.

What's special, for me, is that it feels like having a friendly, wise old man take me by the hand with the words "Why don't we take a break from your busy life and go for a walk? We'll go up a mountain and I'll show you a view. You've probably glimpsed it from time to time, most likely when you weren't looking for it. But today we're going to see the view on purpose. And we'll linger there and spend a while looking at it."

The old man has more to say: "I'm not going to tell you what to do with what you see. I'll just show you the view, and you can look and decide for yourself. You can take it or leave it, as you like. The view is what it is. Then we'll come back down from the mountain and you'll go back to your busy life. But somehow, I don't think you'll forget what you've seen. And you'll be aware the view is always there. What's more, if you let it, this awareness will change how you live your life. Are you ready to come with me?"

How can you resist an invitation like that? So, as we read the words of the *Tao Te Ching*, Lao Tzu takes us by the hand and we go up the mountain together. And he is as good as his word. He does not tell us what to do. He does not even make any suggestions. He simply points things out and makes observations. And his observations are always neutral; he never presents them as though they are right or wrong. He simply observes that when you approach living in a certain way, certain outcomes will likely result. When you approach living in a different way, you will likely get different outcomes. The outcomes are neither good nor bad; they are simply the case.

If Lao Tzu were explaining gravity to a child, he would use words like "Step off high objects and you will fall to the ground. Maybe you'll hurt yourself; maybe you won't. There's nothing wrong with stepping off high objects; but there's no need to be surprised when you fall to the ground every time. By the way, for your information, everyone has decided to call it 'gravity' just so we all know what we're talking about. You're welcome to call it something else if you like, though that will make communication difficult. But what doesn't help is to pretend gravity doesn't exist. It does. It is what it is."

So, we journey up the mountain and Lao Tzu makes his observations along the way. Then we stop, at least for a while, come back down the mountain, and return to the flow of our daily lives. Sometimes we take Lao Tzu's observations to heart. Other times we ignore them or forget them. Either way, just as he promised, we find that what we do is indeed up to us. For me, whenever I reread Lao Tzu's words it's like returning to that journey of amazing insights.

So much for the *Tao Te Ching*. What is this book all about? The idea is simple. This book contains what I imagine might happen if I went for another walk up the same mountain. I have followed the same pattern as in *In Harmony with the Tao*. Each chapter starts with an observation, or series of related observations, and then the rest of the chapter explores what is going on between the lines. But here is the difference:

In my previous book, *In Harmony with the Tao*, the observations at the start of each chapter were Lao Tzu's—I included the entire text of his *Tao Te Ching*, all 81 chapters of it (Stephen Mitchell's version, with kind permission from him and his publisher, HarperCollins). In this book, the observations at the start of each chapter are mine. Some observations are short; others are long. However, I believe we are journeying up the same mountain and that many of the views we will see are the same.

Why take another journey up the same mountain? I think there are four reasons. First, to remind ourselves of what we saw last time, because the views are amazing. Second, to look more closely at certain views for aspects we may have missed first time around. Third, hopefully to catch a glimpse of some new views. Fourth, simply to linger in some favorite places and enjoy what we see.

While Lao Tzu may not be there with us in person, as it were, I hope to bring him along with us in spirit by including many quotes from his *Tao Te Ching*. As in my previous book, these quotes are from Stephen Mitchell's version of the Chinese text. (At the end of each quote, the chapter reference is to the *Tao Te Ching*.) We will use the quotes like trail markers to keep us on track and ensure we do not miss the views.

Two Ways to Read This Book

I think there are basically two ways to undertake a journey. One way is to look at a map ahead of time and then go on the journey. The other way is simply to go on the journey. Each way has its own attractions. I find maps interesting. Of course they are only abstractions, mere representations of reality, but they contain a lot of information in a compact form. You can quickly see the lay of the land and then focus in on whatever interests you. And none of this involves leaving the comfort of your armchair.

However, as the saying goes, "the map is not the territory." Travellers do not study maps; they travel. And there is nothing abstract about going on a journey. It is a very practical matter, and one thing you will definitely have to do is leave the comfort of your armchair. On the other hand, you will experience the journey firsthand for yourself. This experience is, of course, the purpose of travel, and no amount of map-reading will ever provide it. But here is how maps can provide value:

Parts of your journey will likely contain surprises. I think these are of two types: first, the type of surprise that no one could see coming; second, the ones that are not really surprises because you can see them on the map—that is, assuming you look at the map.

This book presents both a journey and a map. And it presents them in that order. You may wonder why I don't present the map first, so we can study it before starting out on the journey. (You might even remind me that surely we could avoid surprises if we did. And you would be right.) But I have decided to start with the journey itself because I think it is more interesting. After all, you don't need a map to enjoy the journey. Sometimes a map is interesting in hindsight, if only to see where you have been.

However, when you look back at the map, it is worth remembering that what you see will be only the abstraction—it will never be the experience. What's more, strictly speaking, it will be only *an* abstraction. This is because other abstractions are possible too. The map will be no more than the mapmaker's idea of where you have been. In contrast, your journey will always be your unique journey, which you experienced firsthand for yourself. No one will be able to tell you otherwise.

So, this book starts with "a journey" and ends with "a map." If you follow this sequence, then when you get to the end, you can look at the map and see if it corresponds to your experience of the journey. Or, if you prefer to start with maps, you can do that instead and then return to the start of the book to go on the journey. It is your choice. Over to you.

I hope you enjoy what lies ahead in this book.

Francis Pring-Mill
Vancouver, BC

PART 1

A JOURNEY

This part of the book is the journey up the mountain. The chapters show the views we see as we stop at various places along the way. Sometimes one view leads naturally into another. In this case, the chapters follow one another. At other times, we travel some distance before we see the next view. So, with that said, let's begin the journey.

1
WHY YOU ARE HERE

You are here to make a difference.
To leave the world a bit better than you found it.
In whatever way you can.

What you have to work with is a set of talents.
They are uniquely yours.
Does it matter where they came from? No.
Does it matter what they are and what you do with them? Yes.
Why?

Because your job is to discover and develop them
and use them to make as much of a positive difference
as possible in the lives of others.
That's all there is to it.
It is not easy but it is simple.

It is not easy because your time is limited.
You get only twenty-four hours a day and one human lifetime.
So you need to focus.
What is easy is to get distracted by details
because there are many things you don't know.

One of them is how long your life will be.
In the end it really doesn't matter,
because at the end you will have run out of time.
That's all you need to know.
Knowing exactly when is a detail because
you can do very little about it.
It's not yours to control.

But what you can do a lot about
is exactly what you do before you die.
This is entirely yours to control.
This is not a detail.
This is what life is all about.
This is why you are here.

Of course, there are constraints.
Of course, it would be nice if many things were different.
Of course, there are many things you don't know.
So what? It doesn't matter.

What matters is to accept what is, as it is, and work with it.
What can you do with things just the way they are?
And the answer is, much more than you think.

Focus.
Resist distraction.
Discover and develop your talents.
Use them every day.
Make a difference.
This is why you are here.

Who am I? What am I doing here? These are the two big questions in life, aren't they? We don't know where we came from, and we don't know where we are going. The only thing we know for sure is that we are here right now. For example, at this very moment you are reading these words. But the two big questions remain. So, what do we do about them? All other things being equal, it seems we get the length of one human lifetime to come up with our answers, or at least to figure out some way to live with the questions.

As a teenager, I had a tough time living with the questions. I felt my life was somehow on hold until I had answers. The *Tao Te Ching* makes many references to being open to the Tao and accepting the world as it is. For example, "If you open yourself to the Tao, you are at one with the Tao and you can embody it completely" (chapter 23); or, "Accept the world as it is. If you accept the world, the Tao will be luminous inside you" (chapter 28). But how could I accept the world without knowing why I was here?

If answers existed, it seemed they were the stuff of religions, and I knew the world had no shortage of those. In fact, there is an amazing variety of religions. Was one of them right? Did that mean the others were wrong? Would I have to study them all, find one that seemed to resonate with me, go with that, and hope I had picked the right one? On the other hand, was there any way it could all be much simpler than that? For example, could I forget about what might be ultimately right or wrong and simply find something good enough for the time being?

This chapter's observation provides an answer. The ideas are not complicated and there is no claim that they are right or wrong. They just suggest an approach that might be good enough for the time being. Looking back on my teenage self, I think that's all I would have needed to get going. Somehow, I cannot help wishing I'd come across these ideas back then; but never mind. Let's explore them now.

The observation starts with "You are here to make a difference. To leave the world a bit better than you found it. In whatever way you can." Well, that's hardly controversial. I doubt any of the world's religions would take exception to that. But it begs the question, What kind of a difference can I make? And so the observation continues with "What you have to work with is a set of talents. They are uniquely yours." As the *Tao Te Ching* reminds us, "Every being in the universe is an expression of the Tao" (chapter 51)—and that includes us.

The observation then anticipates a series of questions we may come up with and provides answers. The answers guide us back on track and help us realize that most of our questions are actually distractions. For example, with respect to our talents, we may wonder, "Does it matter where they came from?" The answer is no. We may wonder, "Does it matter what they are and what you do with them?" The answer is yes. These answers don't leave much to the imagination, do they?

Then we are given an answer to the big question, Why are we here? "Your job is to discover and develop [your talents] and use them to make as much of a positive difference as possible in the lives of others." Nothing more? Is that it? Yes, it is. But we are cautioned, "It is not easy but it is simple." The observation then continues by showing just how easy it is to make things complicated for ourselves.

For example, we may think that our time is limited. Therefore, before we can get going, surely we first need to know when we are going to die. We are told that, yes, our time is limited. But no, we do not need to know when we are going to die. Knowing that each of us has "one human lifetime" is quite enough. Next question?

We might continue with questions like these: Why wasn't I born in another century? Or in a more beautiful body? Or with a more intelligent mind? Or into conditions of wealth and comfort? We can make this list as long as we like. The observation gives the same answer to all these questions: "So what? It doesn't matter." It closes by suggesting that questions like these do nothing but get in the way of making what difference we can make, using what we do have, where we are, right now. In other words, wondering who we might have been or what we might have had are simply further distractions.

How often we think that it would be so much better if things were different. For example, if I was a billionaire philanthropist, then I would be able to do all sorts of wonderful things. But whatever the example is, the trouble always lies with the implication. In this case, the implication is that since I am not a billionaire philanthropist, what little I can do is not worth doing. That is where the trouble lies—right there—because that negative implication is simply not true. What's more, regardless of the example, the negative implication is never true.

Have you ever considered how every time we think, "If only . . .," it represents a huge distraction from the reality of what is? Thoughts like this always take the focus away from what is possible with things exactly the way they are. They do nothing but get in the way of doing what we can with the talents and resources we have (regardless of where they came from). In short, these thoughts are completely beside the point. Why? Because they do nothing toward making a difference in the world. Making a difference—that is the point.

This chapter's observation reminds us, "What matters is to accept what is as it is and work with it." And what can we accomplish? The answer is, "Much more than you think." Therefore, "Focus. Resist distraction. Discover and develop your talents. Use them every day. Make a difference. This is why you are here." That is all you need to know to get going. My teenage self would have loved to have heard those words. It would have saved me a lot of time back then. Come to think of it, those words can still save a lot of time right now.

2
CENTER YOURSELF IN THE TAO

Your actions spring from whatever you're centered in.
You can be centered in your self or centered in the Tao.
Only two places. You choose.

Centered in your self
you will hear nothing but the noise of your own thoughts.
Your actions will spring from desire.
Desire creates expectation.

At best your expectations will be met.
You will experience moments of fleeting satisfaction.
At worst you will experience disappointment.
What's more, these feelings will come and go
as new thoughts and desires spring up
to pull you this way and that.

You will feel separate and apart as you try to stand alone.
You will live in various forms of confusion and sorrow.
You will be at the edge of the circle.

Center your self in the Tao and the noise stops.
You become aware of the Tao continuously unfolding
in endless cycles of expression and renewal.
Desire and expectation will fall away.
You will hear harmony all around you.

Centered in the Tao your actions will spring from the Tao.
At best you will experience pure joy
as you add your unique notes to the music.

At worst you will be carried by the Tao
because no thoughts and desires will pull you this way and that.
Either way you will live in peace and serenity.

These feelings will not come and go,
as there are no fleeting moments in the Tao.
It always was and always will be.
It is going nowhere. It simply is.

You will not feel separate and apart. You will not feel alone.
(You never were—even when you thought you were.)
You will be at the center of the circle.

So, be aware of the Tao. Center yourself in it.
Let the Tao fill the core of your being.
Then let your actions flow from the core of your being.
Forget desire and expectation.
Act with intent and caring.
Listen for the harmony.
Add your own unique notes to the music.

Your actions spring from whatever you're centered in.
Center yourself in the Tao.

One of the themes in the *Tao Te Ching* is balance. As we live our lives, we often disturb this balance and are surprised by the consequences. We do this whenever we wander away from what Lao Tzu refers to as the "center of the circle." Sometimes we wander away unwittingly. Other times we do it on purpose as we try to bend the world to our wishes. The result is always the same—balance is lost. One of my favorite quotes is "The great Way is easy, yet people prefer the side paths. Be aware when things are out of balance. Stay centered within the Tao" (chapter 53).

Wherever we are, it seems natural to see ourselves at the center of the world. After all, it is "our" world. We look out at it from behind our own eyes. The thoughts inside our heads are ours, and we are the ones who act on what we think as we go about living our lives. It seems obvious that we are at the center. However, this observation starts by noting that this is only one of two places where we can be centered. The other place is the Tao. What's more, we are always centered in either one or the other, whether we are aware of it or not. Does it make any difference which place we are centered in? This observation explores an answer.

We start with what happens when we are centered in our self and our thoughts. What follows is a chain reaction of consequences. Thought creates desire. Desire causes action to fulfill desire; it also creates expectation as to the results. Results either meet expectations or they don't. If expectations are met, the best we get is satisfaction. If our expectations are unmet, we get varying degrees of disappointment. And all this comes and goes depending on which desires we chase after in any given moment. "If you let yourself be blown to and fro, you lose touch with your root. If you let restlessness move you, you lose touch with who you are" (chapter 26).

It is not complicated, and the outcome is quite predictable. We feel "separate and apart." We experience "various forms of confusion and sorrow." We live "at the edge of the circle." However, the good news is that it does not have to be this way.

We can also choose to be centered in the Tao. When we do this, the chain reaction that follows is very different. It starts with the absence of any noisy thoughts. No thoughts means no desire. No desire means no expectations. We still act, but our actions are no longer driven by desire; they are no longer a means to an end. Instead, our actions are simply ends in themselves. As such, they are in natural harmony with the Tao in its endless cycles of expression and renewal. In short, our actions are an expression of the Tao, not of our self.

It turns out this makes all the difference in the world. When we add our own unique notes to the music all around us, what we feel is joy. But we do not even have to add our notes. In fact, we do not have to do anything. When we are centered in the Tao, we are simply carried by it regardless of what we do. And there is nowhere better for us to be. "The Tao gives birth to all beings, nourishes them, maintains them, cares for them, comforts them, protects them, takes them back to itself" (chapter 51). "Immersed in the wonder of the Tao, you can deal with whatever life brings you, and when death comes, you are ready" (chapter 11).

What's more, centered in the Tao, we discover we are not separate and apart. We are not alone (we never were). Nothing is coming and going. Life is no longer a struggle. Instead, it is an amazing opportunity to be an expression of the Tao for the length of one human lifetime. We might even become like the Master who "sees things as they are, without trying to control them. She lets them go their own way, and resides at the center of the circle" (chapter 29).

How often we live at the edge of the circle. We think to ourselves that if we chase after one thing or try to hold on to another (or even try to do both at the same time), then surely we will be happy. All we need is a little bit more money, or more security, or to be held in higher esteem by others. It is always our desires that push us to the edge of the circle. And, with the distractions of living in today's busy world, it is easy to spend most of our time there. At the edge of the circle, we think about our actions all the time because they are the only means we have for satisfying our desires.

Have you ever wondered what would happen if you stopped chasing and trying to hold on? What if you could "forget desire and expectation"? What if you did what the Master does? "The Master gives himself up to whatever the moment brings. He . . . has nothing left to hold on to: no illusions in his mind, no resistances in his body. He doesn't think about his actions; they flow from the core of his being" (chapter 50). This is why what is at the core of your being is so important. It makes all the difference.

This chapter's observation reminds us to "let the Tao fill the core of your being. Then let your actions flow from the core of your being." Where you are centered is always what is at the core of your being. And where you are centered is always a matter of choice. "So, be aware of the Tao. Center yourself in it." This may not be easy to do in today's world. But it is simple.

3
LIFE IS RELATIONSHIP

Life is about relationships
with those whom we touch
and those who touch us in the course of our lives.

We touch three groups: family, friends, and a wider group
whose paths we cross, either directly or indirectly without knowing it,
through what we create.

Without relationship we touch no one.
We make no difference.
We might as well not be here.

The only way to touch is through what you do.
So think about it. What will you create?
What consequences will you set in motion?

Your actions will ripple out in space and time
and may continue to touch lives even after you die.
This is the difference you can make.

Life is relationship. It is also short.
While you are here,
be alive.

I remember my school days in a general way, but not many days in particular. However, I remember the day we read John Donne's poem "No Man Is an Island." It was in an English Literature class and I was struck by two things: first, by how true that sentence was; second, by the fact that John Donne had been dead for over three hundred years before I read his words.

I have thought about his poem many times since then. Clearly, we are all connected in some way. John Donne connected with me through his written words. The fact that we have never met (and never will) does not seem to matter. Clearly, space and time have nothing to do with it. So, how does the connection work and what does this mean to us? This observation sees connection in terms of touching (beyond the physical sense) and suggests that as we live our lives, we touch three groups of people.

First, there is our family. Our lives begin with our parents, without whom we would not even be here. Then, as we grow, we become aware of other people around us. Perhaps we have brothers or sisters, so they are family too. Second, there are friends. If there are children next door, we likely play with them and become friends with them. Third, we become aware of a wider group of people out there who are neither family nor friends. We do not even know who they are. Then, as we grow older, we learn that this group of strangers is very large indeed.

Eventually, we learn the world is full of people, each of whom is on their own path just like we are on ours. All that distinguishes family and friends is that our paths cross and we know about it. Typically, we know family and friends by name. What characterizes strangers is that we do not know their names. What's more, most of the time, our paths do not even cross. But sometimes they do. After all, my path crossed with John Donne's.

When paths cross in the same space and time, we touch directly. This happens all the time with the people we know. But when we touch across time, or touch at the same time but across space, then we do so indirectly. Touching across time is what John Donne and I did. Touching across space is what you and I are doing as you read these words (assuming I am still alive). Why does touching matter? Because it is the only way we can make a difference in each other's lives. That is why relationship matters. The observation says, "Without relationship we touch no one. We make no difference. We might as well not be here." Relationship is what life is all about.

The observation describes actions as having ripples across space and time. If you think about it, countless things that affect our lives every day were put there by people who died long ago. For a start, there are all the great works of literature, art, and music. There is the architecture of ancient cathedrals and cities. Everywhere you look are examples of things people did that had lasting consequences. They are all examples of "differences" people made before they died.

However, we do not have to be great composers, artists, or architects to make differences in the lives of others. Nor do the consequences of our actions need to outlive us. We can make differences far closer to home, as it were. But this observation reminds us that our actions are the only means we have for doing so. There is no other way. The only way we can make a difference is through what we do.

In the *Tao Te Ching*, the Master uses actions to make differences—and the way he does so is described as letting in the light. The best way to let in the light is always to step out of the way, to let ourselves go and allow what we do to be all about others. "The Master, by residing in the Tao, sets an example for all beings. Because he doesn't display himself, people can see his light" (chapter 22). "When her work is done, she forgets it. That is why it lasts forever" (chapter 2). "He who clings to his work will create nothing that endures" (chapter 24). In other words, we do not display ourselves; we do not keep reminding others of our good deeds; and we do not cling to what we have done. The Master's actions are never about himself. In the same way, the ripples on the lake from a tossed stone continue long after the stone itself has disappeared below the surface.

How often we act as though we are islands. We do this every time we fail to think about the consequences of our actions, or when we think we are the only ones affected by what we do. If we cannot see a direct connection, we tend to think there is none. But, as we have seen, a connection does not need to be direct to affect others.

Have you ever thought of your actions as rippling out in space and time? Have you ever thought about how far a ripple might go? An action might make a difference right now, if you help an old lady cross the road. But it might alter the course of a life if you sit with a confused child and help him or her see a way forward. It might even make a difference years later if the child, now an adult, remembers your words and uses them to help someone else. There is no telling how far the ripples may go.

This chapter's observation reminds us how much opportunity we have in front of us. "What will you create? What consequences will you set in motion?" We are also reminded that we do not have all the time in the world ahead of us. We have only whatever is left in our particular human life, however long that may be. Hence the closing lines: "Life is relationship. It is also short. While you are here, be alive."

4
WATCH YOUR THOUGHTS

Thoughts need your attention,
preferably your undivided attention.
Without it they go away.

Try watching your thoughts instead of thinking them.
Just watch and see what happens.
Your mind will become empty and silent.

No longer full of anything in particular at any given time,
you become open to everything all at once.
No longer observing and thinking,
you become part of everything.

Then you become aware that even the "part" is a thought.
So, watch that thought until it too goes away.
And now let the watcher go away.

Finally, no longer separate and detached,
you become one with everything.

A thought that does not have your attention is not a thought. This may sound like a joke but it is not. Let's think about it—and that's not a joke either. We all know we have only a certain amount of attention. If we focus on one thing, then that excludes our paying attention to anything else. Attention is like a commodity with a limited supply. Spending more of it here means there is less to spend over there.

This may be fine as long as we are the ones doing the spending. But we have likely all had the experience of thoughts taking us places we do not want to go. For example, we somehow find ourselves worrying nonproductively about some aspect of the future or regretting something in the past that cannot be undone. Why do we do this? Are we having our thoughts, or are our thoughts "having" us, as it were? Who is in charge? This is a good question.

The *Tao Te Ching* has a lot to say about thoughts. Sometimes thought is useful. For example, "Prevent trouble before it arises. Put things in order before they exist" (chapter 64). Putting things in order requires thinking clearly about what you are doing. But, at other times, thought can create trouble instead of preventing it. Rather than produce clarity, thoughts can also muddy the waters. "Do you have the patience to wait till your mud settles and the water is clear?" (chapter 15). Thus thought can produce mixed results. So, what is the solution? Is there a way to enjoy the benefits while avoiding the risks?

The *Tao Te Ching* suggests there is—and it is quite simple. "Stop thinking and end your problems" (chapter 20). Or "Empty your mind of all thoughts. Let your heart be at peace" (chapter 16). This sounds like a great idea, except that when we try to do this in practice, we find it is not so simple. How exactly do we "empty our mind of all thoughts"? This question is what this observation addresses.

We started by noting that if you do not pay attention to a thought, then it does not exist. This suggests that if we deny attention from a thought, it will literally "go away." This insight is the key. This observation suggests, "Try watching your thoughts instead of thinking them." Instead of giving attention to your thoughts, detach yourself from them. Stand apart from them. "Just watch and see what happens." You will find that "your mind will become empty and silent." If thoughts are like noisy little creatures clamoring for your attention, then when they are starved of attention, the noise stops and they disappear. It is as simple as that.

Now something very interesting happens. "No longer full of anything in particular at any given time, you become open to everything all at once." What is happening here? We saw earlier that your attention is no longer yours when you give it to some thought in particular. What's more, as long as you are having one thought, you cannot have another. Thought limits you to one thing at a time. So, at least for a while, your mind is now both closed and full.

This is why, when you take your attention back again, instead of being closed, "you become open to everything all at once." You no longer have different thoughts about different things at different moments in time, and it is as though time has ceased to exist. This is why you become open "all at once." Also, because you are no longer making thought-based distinctions between things, it is also as though everything has ceased to exist as separate things. Everything has become one "thing," as it were. There is no separation, only Oneness/Wholeness. This is why "no longer observing and thinking, you become part of everything." This is what is happening.

In fact, even being "part of everything" is a thought, because Oneness/Wholeness has no parts. What do we do with that thought? The same thing we did before: "So, watch that thought until it too goes away." What are we left with now? We are left with only the watcher. So, the last step is to let the watcher go away. And what is the result? "Finally, no longer separate and detached, you become one with everything." Even the you that was doing the thinking has now disappeared. What happened? In letting go of thought, you revealed awareness. It was there all along, just like Oneness/Wholeness.

How often we put our trust in thought. Thought is how we make distinctions. We separate things from one another by naming them. As the *Tao Te Ching* says, "Naming is the origin of all particular things" (chapter 1). The trouble is, we do not stop there. Not content with identifying and naming things, our mind goes on to have further thoughts about them. We decide some "particular things" are to be desired and others are to be avoided. Some are to be hoped for and others are to be feared. We have opinions about things and make judgments about them. What's more, we do the same with other people. With so much to think about, it is hardly surprising we often muddy the waters!

Have you ever considered how, in the world of awareness, there are no distinctions? This is why, when we are completely open-minded, we become "one with everything." No longer thought-bound, we discover we are also no longer time-bound. This is why we are not only open to everything; we are also open to it all at once. The Master is aware of this. What's more, he recognizes this is the value of getting away from the distractions of everyday life. "Ordinary men hate solitude. But the Master makes use of it, embracing his aloneness, realizing he is one with the whole universe" (chapter 42).

This chapter's observation reminds us we are always one with the whole universe. The trouble is that we keep thinking we are separate and apart. The trouble is, we keep thinking!

5
JUST BE

Allow yourself to just be.
Be content with just being.
Forget your self with all its strivings
and just become part of beingness.

Don't worry, you will still get things done.
But results will flow from alignment with general harmony
rather than from effort applied to achieving particular goals.

Think beingness and alignment
instead of effort and goals.
Think flow instead of striving.
And now, don't think at all.

Just be.

The *Tao Te Ching* suggests, "Be content with what you have; rejoice in the way things are" (chapter 44). Why is it that we do not generally have time for this? The answer is, because we are usually too busy striving. Of course, there are the daily activities of human living. But once basic needs are met, we typically chase after a great deal more. What is it we are striving for? We are usually striving for more of something. Examples include money, security, material possessions, and the esteem of others. We tend to think that once we have got those, then we will be content. So, in the meantime, we do not "rejoice in the way things are." Instead, we hold off until things are the way we want them to be.

Where do our strivings originate? The answer is, they always originate in the same place: the self. Here's how it works. First, the self imagines a version of reality other than the one that is here right now. Then it judges the imaginary version to be better than the real thing. Then the self desires the "better" version and starts striving to make it so. It is an interesting process, isn't it? Striving always requires standing separate and apart from the present moment and making judgments about it—and only the self can do that.

In contrast, to "just be" requires nothing to be other than the way it is. No judgment is called for. No commentary from your self is needed. In fact, your self gets in the way. This observation suggests, "Forget your self with all its strivings and just become part of beingness." Your self is not involved. No standing separate and apart. No striving. Just being. And what is the result? As the *Tao Te Ching* observes of the Master, "Because she has let go of herself, she is perfectly fulfilled" (chapter 7). As for imaginary better versions of the way things are, you recognize they are no more than illusions. "The Master . . . dwells in reality, and lets all illusions go" (chapter 38).

Does this mean the self is useless? No. Can we still get things done? Yes. The question is whether we take direction from our self or from the Tao. When we take direction from our self, we start focusing on achieving particular goals. This means we have particular outcomes or results in mind and strive to bring them about. But when we take direction from the Tao, then something different happens.

When we take direction from the Tao we do not start with our self and our desires. Instead, we start by listening. We become aware of reality just as it is, unfolding in the present moment exactly the way it does. We do not stand separate and apart. We do not compare reality with some imaginary better version of itself, judge it as falling short in one way or another, and then start work to reshape it. We simply listen. Then, when our thoughts fall silent, we hear a harmony that is always there. And we become aware of a picture that is far bigger than any we can imagine.

"In harmony with the Tao, the sky is clear and spacious, the earth is solid and full, all creatures flourish together, content with the way they are, endlessly repeating themselves, endlessly renewed" (chapter 39). At this level, there are no particular outcomes and results to desire. There are no goals to strive for and achieve. If people centered themselves in the Tao, then they "would be content with their simple everyday lives, in harmony, and free of desire." (chapter 37). At first, we may think that means we would not do anything. However, this is not so. We still very much have a part to play. We each have our own unique song to sing. The difference is that we start by aligning ourselves with the harmony that is already there, and then we sing our song. When we start with ourselves, all we create is noise and confusion.

To listen is to no longer have a better version of reality in mind. Instead, we let go of whatever we were thinking. We do not have anything in mind at all. When we do this, the striving stops and we make an amazing discovery—actions become effortless. "The Master gives himself up to whatever the moment brings. He ... has nothing left to hold on to: no illusions in his mind, no resistances in his body. He doesn't think about his actions; they flow from the core of his being" (chapter 50). And we can do this any time we choose. This is the difference between endless striving and serenity.

How often we are not content with just being. We are so used to striving and chasing after goals that we think to do anything else amounts to a waste of time. We might even look at the notion of beingness and wonder what kind of a goal that is and how we might strive after it.

Have you ever had the experience of seeming to create something almost without effort? Whatever you needed seemed to appear at just the right time. Your actions produced exactly the result you wanted with no need for correction. You were present and involved, but somehow it seemed all you did was guide and shape something that was happening anyway. Could this be because you adopted the Master's approach? "Because he has no goal in mind, everything he does succeeds" (chapter 22).

This chapter's observation reminds us to "think beingness and alignment instead of effort and goals. Think flow instead of striving." And it all starts with listening. And listening starts with letting go of our thoughts. So let's do that. Hence the final words:

"And now, don't think at all. Just be."

6
LET THE LIGHT SHINE

Enlightenment is like a flash of light
in which you see everything just as it is
without the interference of thought.

Suddenly you are aware
the light is inside you and all around you
and in every separate thing you think you see.

The flash catches your attention
but the light is there all the time.
And you can live in it all the time.

Just let go of your attachment to any thought of separateness,
including yourself as something separate from everything else.
Let go of your attachment to thought itself.
Just let the light shine.

The *Tao Te Ching* makes many references to light. "Can you cleanse your inner vision until you see nothing but the light?" (chapter 10). "The Master arrives without leaving, sees the light without looking, achieves without doing a thing" (chapter 47). "Use your own light to return to the source of light" (chapter 52).

However, our experience tells us that most of the time we do not see the light. We certainly do not see the light "without looking." In fact, even when we look, we often still do not see it. Much of the time it seems we live our lives in varying shades of darkness. Some days nothing seems to make any sense and it feels as though darkness is just the way it is. We feel separate and apart and are not quite sure what we are doing here.

But it is not always like this. Every so often we see a flash of light. For a brief instant, we become aware of something vastly bigger than ourselves that cannot be described in words. Suddenly it feels as though we are no longer separate and apart. Instead, we experience a Oneness/Wholeness that is everything all together, all at once, including us. "It is serene. Empty. Solitary. Unchanging. Infinite. Eternally present. It is the mother of the universe. For lack of a better name, I call it the Tao" (chapter 25).

This is the light that the Master sees. In fact, this is where he lives all the time. "The Master, by residing in the Tao, sets an example for all beings. Because he doesn't display himself, people can see his light" (chapter 22). Even when we cannot see it, the light is always there—including inside ourselves. The reason we can see it in the Master is that he does not let the self get in the way. What that means for us is that if we want to see the light and live in it, all we need do is follow his example.

The *Tao Te Ching* suggests there is only one thing that blocks the light, and that is our self. And most of the time, unless we are aware of it, we are full of ourselves. The reason we do not see the light in ourselves, or in our experience of the world, is that our self and our thoughts get in the way. However, the good news is that the flash does succeed in catching our attention. When it happens, it is undeniable. The flash reminds us the light is there all the time whether we see it or not. So, how can we see the light all the time and live in it like the Master does?

The answer is to pay close attention to our thoughts. At all times, there is only one question to ask: Is our mind centered in our self or centered in the Tao? Centered in our self we hear nothing but the noise of our own thoughts and we block the light. "The Master keeps her mind always at one with the Tao; that is what gives her her radiance" (chapter 21). How does she do that? The answer is that she recognizes that the self is the origin of all thoughts, so she lets go of her self. "The Master . . . is detached from all things; that is why she is one with them. Because she has let go of herself, she is perfectly fulfilled" (chapter 7).

The message is clear. When we let go of our self, we let go of our thoughts. When we let go of our thoughts, we no longer see ourselves as separate and apart. No longer separate and apart, we no longer block the light. We let the light shine. It is as simple as that.

How often we look for light in all the wrong places. When things do not make sense, we feel like we are in the dark. We even use the phrase "shed light" when we use thought to try to make sense of things. We think light comes from understanding, and understanding comes from making sense of things, and making sense of things comes from thinking about them. And so we try harder.

What if light is beyond understanding? What if light has nothing to do with whether or not we succeed in making sense of things? What if to see the light, we need to do nothing more than be aware and accept things exactly the way they are? When we sit in awe of an amazing sunset there is no need for thought. There is no need to understand the sunset, or make sense of it, or judge it, or comment on it, or compare it with other sunsets, or have opinions about it. The sunset is what it is and we simply experience it. We let go of thought. We let go of our self. There is nothing between us and the sunset. Just Oneness/Wholeness.

Of course, there is more to life than watching sunsets. If only life was that easy, you might say. But this observation suggests that letting go of our self and our thoughts, opinions, and judgments can reduce the noise and confusion that blocks the light. We do not even need to compare our thoughts with each other, evaluate them, and keep some and reject others as we try to make sense of them. It is much simpler than that.

This chapter's observation reminds us that letting go is all it takes to let the light shine.

7
LIVING IN AWARENESS

Let your self go.
Become aware of the Oneness/Wholeness of everything.
Realize that the separateness of all things is merely apparent
    and not real.
This is to experience enlightenment.
And it can happen in a moment.

To live your daily life in this awareness,
simply accept that this is reality and that everything else is illusion.
The illusion appears real because it is based on our senses.
But we can accept this apparent reality without believing it
and without acting as if it is real.
When we do, we live in peace and serenity.
When we don't, we live in various forms of confusion and sorrow.
And we make the choice with every moment of every day.

So, how do we take moments of enlightenment
and stretch them across hours, days, months, and years of living?

If we do the following it seems to help.
Live in constant awareness of apparent reality as an illusion.
Let go of attachment to any apparently separate "thing."
Have faith in the Oneness/Wholeness of everything.
Use action to help the unfolding of everything without interfering.
They call this "moving in the world while dwelling in the Tao."

Enlightenment can happen in a single moment.
But living in harmony with reality is something to be done
afresh again and again with every moment of every day.

This observation picks up where the last one left off. In the last observation ("Let the Light Shine"), we saw how "The Master, by residing in the Tao, sets an example for all beings. Because he doesn't display himself, people can see his light" (chapter 22). He "dwells in reality, and lets all illusions go" (chapter 38). This observation asks the question, How exactly does he do that? How do we reside in the Tao, dwell in reality, and let all illusions go?

The reason we do not dwell in reality most of the time is that we see ourselves as separate. We think we are on the inside and there is a world "out there" that we interact with. As far as we can tell, this is the way reality is, and our five senses give us lots of supporting evidence. Apparently, there are thousands of separate things out there, and they all seem real because we can see them, hear them, smell them, taste them, touch them—and, of course, name them and talk about them. As far as we are concerned, this is as real as it gets.

However, this is to make a big assumption, which is that what we can see is all there is. While this is certainly the reality we experience, is it the only one? The reality we experience is also something that comes and goes and changes. It appears to be temporary, and constant only in its change. The *Tao Te Ching* describes a different eternal reality like this: "There was something formless and perfect before the universe was born. It is serene. Empty. Solitary. Unchanging. Infinite. Eternally present. It is the mother of the universe. For lack of a better name, I call it the Tao" (chapter 25).

Whatever this reality is, it does not come or go or change. In fact, it does not look like anything we can see, hear, smell, taste, or touch. What's more, being formless, it does not even consist of separate parts we can name and talk about. All we can do is point at it with words like "for lack of a better name." If this is the Tao, then what is it, and how do we dwell in it?

The *Tao Te Ching* suggests that to dwell in the Tao, we need to let go of words and thoughts. In fact, we need to let go of the pursuit of knowledge, which aims to name things and pin them down in a structure we can get our heads around. (Actually, to be fair, the words in the *Tao Te Ching* never suggest we "need" to do anything. The words simply point out what tends to happen when we make certain choices. And pursuing knowledge is a choice.) Instead, it suggests we replace the pursuit of knowledge with simple awareness—nothing more complicated than that. When we live in awareness, we live in harmony with the Tao, and we discover that words are not needed. This is what the Master does. "Teaching without words, performing without actions: that is the Master's way" (chapter 43). So, how does he do it?

This observation suggests the way to do it is to accept the apparent reality that our five senses tell us about, while at the same time remembering that it is no more than an illusion. In other words, we accept the illusion but we do not believe that it is real—and, more important, we do not act *as if* it is real. "The Master observes the world but trusts his inner vision" (chapter 12). When we do this, we live our lives centered in the Tao, and we experience peace and serenity. On the other hand, when we live centered in the illusion, we join what the *Tao Te Ching* calls the "turmoil of beings" and experience various forms of "confusion and sorrow." This amounts to living in the dark instead of living in the light.

But, at a practical level, how do we remind ourselves of the illusion? How do we live in awareness and in the light on a day-to-day basis? This observation gives four suggestions. The first suggestion is to remain constantly aware that apparent reality is no more than an illusion. This means we accept the illusion but are not drawn into it, as it were; we do not center ourselves in it. The second suggestion is to remember that in the Tao there are no separate "things." To form any attachments to them is therefore to be drawn into the illusion, to believe and act as if the "things" are real. We need to guard against this, and awareness of attachment is a useful warning sign.

The third suggestion is to "have faith in the Oneness/Wholeness of everything." This is to let go and to trust the Tao, instead of putting our faith in our so-called knowledge about all the separate things we think we see. The fourth suggestion builds on this by reminding us that when we see ourselves as separate, we tend to use our actions to bend the world to our wishes, which often amounts to little more than interfering. When we no longer see ourselves as separate, then our actions become part of the natural unfolding of everything and we live in the flow.

How often we live inside the illusion. All we see is the separateness of things. We name them, organize them, make judgments about them, chase after some and avoid others. What's more, we make judgments about other people based on what they do. Inside the illusion, our lives quickly become complicated and, needless to say, harmony and light often disappear.

Can you remember the last time you stepped outside the illusion? It would have felt like having no preconceived idea of how anything should unfold. You would have had no attachments to anything, would not have minded what happened, would have been completely at peace with reality exactly the way it was. This is what trust looks like. This is to have faith in the Oneness/Wholeness of everything. Your actions would have felt effortless. You would have been "moving in the world while dwelling in the Tao."

This chapter's observation reminds us that living in awareness is a choice, but it is not a one-time choice. It is "something to be done afresh again and again with every moment of every day."

8
LET GO

Let go of your desire for things to be a certain way.
And simply accept what is as it is
without desiring that it be any different.

This does not mean you do not care one way or another.
Nor does it mean you have no goals.
It simply means you desire no particular outcome
and expect no particular result.

Desire and expectation are not needed.
What's more, they interfere
because they linger once you have acted.
They are your vested interest
in a particular outcome or a particular result.
They prevent you from letting go.

Only the opportunity to influence is yours.
You don't get to control the detailed consequences.
So let your goal be no more than a creative intent
to shape the unfolding of what is about to be.

Aim to create harmony.
Forget desire and expectation.
Act with intent and caring.
Then let go.

The *Tao Te Ching* makes many references to letting go. "The Master . . . is detached from all things; that is why she is one with them. Because she has let go of herself, she is perfectly fulfilled" (chapter 7). "Do your work, then step back. The only path to serenity" (chapter 9). "If you want to accord with the Tao, just do your job, then let go" (chapter 24). "Nothing is impossible for him. Because he has let go, he can care for the people's welfare as a mother cares for her child" (chapter 59).

Why is it that we do not let go? Think of all the benefits. We could be "one with all things." We could be "perfectly fulfilled." We could be on the "path to serenity." We could "care for the people's welfare as a mother cares for her child." Who would not want to be able to do all that? I think there are two reasons why we do not let go.

The first is that we do not accept things as they are; and the reason we do not do that is that we desire that they be a certain way. If the world does not measure up, then we see it as our job to go in and fix it. From our perspective, it is not our thoughts that fail to align with reality—it is reality that fails to align with our thoughts. Faced with the choice between accepting things as they are or holding on to our version of the way we want them to be, we tend to hold on to our version.

I think the second reason we do not let go is because we tend to think of acceptance as something passive. We think acceptance means not doing anything at all, acting as if we do not have any part to play in the unfolding of "the way things are." We may think that amounts to not caring. But here's the question: What is it that we are caring about? Are we caring about ourselves and our desires, or are we caring about the world? The *Tao Te Ching* reminds us the Master "cares about nothing but the Tao. Thus he can care for all things" (chapter 64). So how does the Master succeed in doing this, and where do we go astray?

I think desire starts with not accepting things the way they are, and deciding to reshape them. This often becomes a project with goals to be achieved. The focus is on the future, and we see the present as no more than the means for getting from here to there. What's more, we now have an expectation of what things will look like when we get there and have achieved our goal. We are looking for a particular outcome, a particular result, and the whole purpose of the project is to bring it about. As this observation points out, this expectation becomes our "vested interest" in what we are doing.

The trouble with this approach is that we act as if we are in control when, typically, we are not. Most of the time, what happens is not entirely up to us. In reality, as opposed to in our minds, "Only the opportunity to influence is yours. You don't get to control the detailed consequences." So, what does this mean for our goals?

I think all it means is that we let go of what we cannot control and look for opportunities to contribute to something bigger than whatever we had in mind. To do that, the first thing we need to let go of is our vested interest. So, instead of clinging to our desires and expectations, we do what the Master does. "The Master allows things to happen. She shapes events as they come. She steps out of the way and lets the Tao speak for itself" (chapter 45). The difference lies in who is doing the speaking (is it us or the Tao?) and whether or not we step out of the way so the Tao can speak for itself.

When we let go of expectation and accept that shaping is not the same as controlling, then we become free to participate in the creation of something far greater than any goal we can imagine. "Have faith in the way things are. Love the world as your self; then you can care for all things" (chapter 13).

How often we pick small goals. We like to get our head around all the details and be in control of making things happen our way. It is as if we think reality is a lump of clay, useless in its current form but with potential to be fashioned into something useful.

Have you ever thought about reality not as something to be fashioned into anything, but instead as something to be experienced just the way it is? We have to admit, reality does a pretty good job of unfolding all on its own; it really does not need us to help it along. What if our part is to listen and then, having listened, to respond? Simply to contribute our unique talents to what is unfolding anyway and to let go of our idea of exactly what the result should look like.

This chapter's observation reminds us of the bigger picture and how to recognize our part in it. "Aim to create harmony. Forget desire and expectation. Act with intent and caring. Then let go." That is all it takes.

9
TO SEE LIGHT

To see light, be still.
To hear harmony, be aware.
To create order, be focused.
To reveal simplicity, be patient.
To bring peace, be compassionate.

Light. Stillness.
Harmony. Awareness.
Order. Focus.
Simplicity. Patience.
Peace. Compassion.

See.
Hear.
Create.
Reveal.
Bring.

Be.

It seems to me Lao Tzu summarizes the entire *Tao Te Ching* in three words when he says, "I have just three things to teach: simplicity, patience, compassion. These three are your greatest treasures" (chapter 67). He also points out that living these three treasures in our daily lives has nothing to do with the words themselves. "Teaching without words, performing without actions: that is the Master's way" (chapter 43).

This observation explores what we need to do to live in harmony with the Tao. But first, I should note that "need" is not a neutral word. (Words can be tricky, which is why the Master prefers to avoid them.) In reality, of course, we do not "need" to do anything. We are always living in the Tao whether we are aware of it or not. However, there are some things we can learn from the Master. One of these is that "he doesn't think about his actions; they flow from the core of his being" (chapter 50). What matters is not so much what we do but where we are coming from when we do it. So, if we want our actions to flow, how do we align the "core of our being" with the Tao?

I think the word "being" is the clue. For example, we might think that to see light, we need to look for it. If we do not find it wherever we first look, then we might think we are looking in the wrong place. So we should look in other places. But the first line in this observation suggests that this is not the way to go. Instead, it says, to see light we need simply to "be still." Similarly, to hear harmony we might think we need to listen for it. But the second line suggests all we need do is "be aware."

How does being still and being aware allow us to see light and hear harmony? I think the answer lies in that they are not actions we perform; they are states of being. The Master lives in harmony with the Tao simply by living in a state of awareness. "He has no will of his own. He dwells in reality, and lets all illusions go" (chapter 38).

Although our thoughts often tend to get in the way, there is a role for thought. "Prevent trouble before it arises. Put things in order before they exist" (chapter 64). Thought can be a useful tool for putting things in order. But we need to remember not to let it run the show all the time. Hence this observation suggests, "To create order, be focused." This acknowledges that thought is useful at certain times; it just needs to be kept in its place.

Often our world seems complicated and we think that simplifying it involves an act of will. Sometimes it does. But this observation makes another suggestion, once again based in being rather than action: "To reveal simplicity, be patient." This suggests that simplicity is there all the time, and complexity is something we layer on top of it. The *Tao Te Ching* suggests that much of the time this layering amounts to no more than mud. "Do you have the patience to wait till your mud settles and the water is clear?" (chapter 15). The clue is patience. Lastly, this observation picks up on the third of Lao Tzu's three treasures: "To bring peace, be compassionate." And, like awareness and patience, compassion is another state of being.

If we think of light, harmony, order, simplicity, and peace as elements, then the next few lines match these elements to states of being. These states are stillness, awareness, focus, patience, and compassion. What is important is that these states of being are things we can choose. The next few lines show what these choices look like in terms of the verbs describing our actions. These verbs are "see," "hear," "create," "reveal," and "bring." We sometimes talk about "where the action is." These verbs are where the action is, if you like. But all of them share a common foundation. And this is simply the state of dwelling in harmony with the Tao—a state of awareness which consists of "being." "When nothing is done, nothing is left undone. True mastery can be gained by letting things go their own way" (chapter 48). Being, not doing—this is "true mastery." Hence the last line of the observation is simply the word "be." That says it all.

How often we do not live in light and harmony, as it were. Our days sometimes feel dark, and we hear noise and discord rather than harmony. There is a well-known saying that goes like this: We think we need to *have* certain things so we can *do* what we want, and then we will *be* happy. We think the sequence goes first have, then do, then be. The saying continues by reminding us that this is back-to-front. In reality, as opposed to in our minds, the sequence goes first be, then do, then have. In other words, first *be* who you are, then *do* what comes naturally to you, and you will end up *having* all you need. The point is, it all starts with be—it doesn't end with be.

Have you ever felt that to experience light and harmony in your life depended on your "having" certain things? And that to have those things, there were certain things you had to "do"? For example, you had to get the right college qualification, work for some number of years doing a job, earn enough money to have a certain kind of house, find the right relationship with someone. Then, and only then, would you "be" happy, content, and at peace. To believe this is to spend your life endlessly striving for one thing after another after another. What if, instead of doing and striving, it all starts with being?

This chapter's observation reminds us we can choose our states of being any time we want. We do not need to wait for anything. And when we choose these states of being, our actions become the natural expression of them, and we end up having in our life whatever things we really need. It's all much simpler than we think. Striving is not required. It all starts with being.

10
LISTEN FOR THE HARMONY

Listen for the harmony
and sing your part in it.
Feel the rhythm
and move with the dance.
See beyond the differences
and embrace the Oneness.
Look for the light
and embody the brightness.

Harmony. Dance.
Oneness. Brightness.

Sing.
Move.
Embrace.
Embody.

The *Tao Te Ching* makes many references to harmony. "In harmony with the Tao, the sky is clear and spacious, the earth is solid and full, all creatures flourish together, content with the way they are" (chapter 39). If we could "remain centered in the Tao, all things would be in harmony. The world would become a paradise. All people would be at peace" (chapter 32). If to live in harmony with the Tao is to flourish, be content, enjoy paradise, and be at peace, then why don't we do this all the time?

I think there are two reasons. Let's look at each in turn. The first reason is that we do not hear the harmony. And we do not hear it because we do not listen for it. Too often our minds are full of the sound of our own thoughts. Thoughts demand attention and can be very noisy. In fact, if we are not careful, they can easily drown out everything else. This is why to hear anything we first have to be quiet. There is no other way. Once we are quiet, then we can listen for the harmony. And when we do, we discover that it is always there (it always was there). That is why this observation opens with "Listen for the harmony."

The second reason we do not live in harmony with the Tao is because we do not respond to what we hear. I think the way to respond to harmony is to recognize we have a part and sing it. We can sing literally if we want to, but I'm thinking of singing as a metaphor for acting in harmony with something much bigger than whatever desires and expectations we may happen to have in our heads at any moment. I think each of us has a unique song to sing, a special part to play. After all, we are all uniquely different from one another. Every song has the potential to contribute. And we sing our song every day in the way we live our lives.

If singing is the music, then movement is the dance. "Feel the rhythm and move with the dance." However, much of the time we do not dance. Instead, we march to the sound of our own thoughts. We have plans, goals, and objectives, and we see the purpose of our actions as being to direct and control. Dance is different. Like singing, it is a response to harmony. And it starts not with analyzing and planning, but with awareness and feeling.

The next lines remind us that the harmony we are listening and responding to is at the level of "the Oneness." This simply means it is beyond thought—nothing more than that. We may recall, thought works by naming things so we can distinguish them from one another. This is why words fail when we try to talk about the Tao. "The tao that can be told is not the eternal Tao" (chapter 1). As soon as we name it and talk about it, we fail. It does not matter what name we give it; we fail every time. "The name that can be named is not the eternal Name. The unnamable is the eternally real. Naming is the origin of all particular things," (chapter 1) and the Tao is clearly not a "particular thing." This observation uses the word "Oneness" to point to the unnamable eternal reality that is the Tao. This is why it says, "See beyond the differences and embrace the Oneness."

The observation continues, "Look for the light and embody the brightness." We may recall that the Master, dwelling in the Tao, "sees the light without looking" (chapter 47). However, most of the time, we do not see the light. And the reason we do not see it is because we are looking somewhere outside ourselves. The light is inside. That is where we need to look. "Use your own light and return to the source of light. This is called practicing eternity" (chapter 52). The *Tao Te Ching* gives us all the clues we need.

The next lines summarize the four things to focus on: harmony, dance, Oneness, and brightness. And the final lines summarize our response with the four actions we can take: sing, move, embrace, and embody. In short, living in harmony with the Tao is all about listening and responding.

How often we live inside our own heads. What we listen to, and take direction from, are our thoughts and desires. When we start by listening to the Tao, we hear a harmony that is there all the time. To take direction from the Tao is simply to align ourselves with it. It's no more complicated than that. When we do this, we see beyond the differences. We stop making judgments. We stop accepting some things and rejecting others depending on whether they suit our purposes. "The Master ... is ready to use all situations and doesn't waste anything. This is called embodying the light" (chapter 27).

Have you ever acted without intent to fulfill a desire or an expectation? We sometimes use the phrase "go with the flow," but we seldom first listen for the flow, align ourselves with it, and then see what happens. Why not? Do we not trust it? Would we rather trust ourselves? When we trust the flow, the results can be surprising. We can find ourselves contributing in ways we had not even imagined. What's more, at times our actions seem effortless. It is as though we are being carried by the flow of something much bigger than we are, at the same time that we are actively involved in creating it.

This chapter's observation reminds us that listening for the harmony calls for a response. When we respond, we may feel carried by the flow, but our response is not a passive one—it is active. Specifically, our response is to sing with the harmony, move with the dance, embrace the Oneness, and embody the brightness.

11
POINT OF VIEW

We think our point of view brings detachment,
enabling us to observe reality as it is.
After all, you cannot see something if you stand too close.
You need distance between yourself and what you want to see.
Without detachment you cannot see it objectively.
You cannot see it for what it really is. Or so we think.
For this is to see with the eye of thought.

What if all separation is illusion and only unity is real?
What if in reality there is no distance between you and
 anything else?
What if there are no "things" and all your distinctions are illusions?
What if there is only Oneness/Wholeness?

If this is true, then to see with the eye of thought
is to be unaware that thought itself
creates the distance between us and what we want to see.
After all, without distance we would be one with what
 we want to see.
We could not think about it because we would be it.
This beingness would be reality.
What thought creates would be illusion.

To see if this is true, just let go of your thoughts
 and see what happens.
You will discover your point of view disappears.
So does distance. So does separation.

All that remains is Oneness/Wholeness.
It included you before you started thinking,
while you thought, and when you stopped thinking.
It was always there even while you thought you were separate.

We think our point of view brings detachment,
enabling us to observe reality as it is.
But instead it brings attachment to our point of view.
We gain distance and separation.
But we step into illusion.
We lose reality.

We value truth and spend much of our time seeking it. When we believe we have found it, we often subject it to various tests to ensure it is indeed "objectively" true. This thinking has many useful applications. This is how we explore our world and build what we call "knowledge" about it.

Indeed, science works by proving or disproving ideas about what we call the truth of things. And not everything we think is true withstands the test. Some things turn out to be what we call false. Science is the disciplined business of sifting, sorting, and organizing the results of these tests. As the *Tao Te Ching* reminds us, "In the pursuit of knowledge, every day something is added" (chapter 48). And we have managed to add a lot over the centuries.

But this approach assumes there is such a thing as objective truth and that we have to stand back to see it. In other words, it assumes that things really are a certain way and that if we stand too close, then we cannot see them for what they really are. These are big assumptions and this observation questions them.

What follows is a string of "What if . . . ?" questions, one after another. They focus on the basis of our whole truth-seeking approach. If the answers to the questions are true, then every time we go seeking the truth, it would seem that we miss it. That is not to say we do not find anything useful—we often do. But it is to put what we find into a context that is much more limited than we tend to think it is.

This observation says that "to see with the eyes of thought is to be unaware that thought itself creates the distance between us and what we want to see." So, does this mean that all objective truths are artifacts of our mind? The short answer is yes. Is this a problem? The short answer is no, as long as we remember that we are not looking at anything eternally real. What's more, we can still do useful things with the results. But what we are looking at is an illusion nonetheless. So, how does the illusion work?

When we are so close to something that we cannot distinguish it from ourselves, we do not see it as something separate. Only when we stand back and put some distance between us and it can we see it as an "it." We are here and "it" is there. We can point at "it" and give it a name. This exercise is fine as long as we do not kid ourselves that we are pointing at anything eternally real. As the *Tao Te Ching* reminds us, "The name that can be named is not the eternal Name. The unnamable is the eternally real. Naming is the origin of all particular things" (chapter 1). So, how do we see the eternally real?

The answer is to stand further back. And when we have done that, to stand back even further still. Imagine yourself having identified a needle in a haystack and now zooming back so far that you are looking at the world from space. You cannot see the needle now, can you? All you can see is the world in its oneness and wholeness.

Now, you might say all that has changed is your scale. Instead of needles in haystacks, you can now see not only the world from space but also other planets and stars that you could not see before (because your head was in the haystack). Most likely you will now promptly forget about the world in its oneness and wholeness and start pointing at the other planets and stars and naming them instead. As it were, they become the needles in the new haystack of space. Thought always focuses on the needles.

This observation suggests that the way to zoom back to the level of eternal reality is to let go of your thoughts entirely. When you do that, "you will discover your point of view disappears. So does distance. So does separation." What do you see now? "All that remains is Oneness/Wholeness." You are looking at something on a scale so big you can no longer identify it as "something." It is so big that the words "big" and "scale" do not even apply. What we are trying to talk about is the eternal Tao—and we are failing. "The tao that can be told is not the eternal Tao" (chapter 1).

This is the Oneness/Wholeness that "included you before you started thinking, while you thought, and when you stopped thinking. It was always there even while you thought you were separate." Points of view are fine as far as they go. They can even produce "objective," testable truths; they can help us organize and control our world. But, in the grand scheme of things, they do not go very far; they are no more than superficial and pretty. "Therefore the Master concerns himself with the depths and not the surface, with the fruit and not the flower.... He dwells in reality, and lets all illusions go" (chapter 38).

How often we pride ourselves on standing back to "see the big picture" and believe we are looking at things as they really are. We believe we are looking at what the Master calls "the depths" and the "fruit and not the flower." How ironic that in our detachment we fail to see our attachment to our point of view. For all our so-called objectivity, we are still dwelling inside the illusion. In the big picture, it turns out our point of view not only fails to go very far—it also disappears completely.

Have you ever simply let go of your thoughts and watched your point of view disappear? It disappears the moment thought stops. It does so because suddenly there is no distance, there is no separation. Without separation, there can be no thought. There is no room for it. In fact, there is no you—because "you" is just another thought.

This chapter's observation reminds us that when we let go of thought, we step out of the illusion. It is when we do this that we step into reality. If eternal truth is what we value, then reality is the place to dwell.

12
FREEDOM FROM DESIRE

To desire is to instantly create two obstacles.
First, separation between you and whatever you desire.
If you already possessed what you desire, there would be
    no separation.
Second, attachment to the object of your desire.
It now represents something you want but do not yet have.

Thus, to the degree you desire,
you are both separated and attached.
You are no longer free.
You are imprisoned by desire.
Your actions are dictated by desire.

But freedom can be yours in an instant.
Simply accept the world just as it is
without desiring that it be any different.
Suddenly separation will be gone, attachment will vanish,
and the prison walls will disappear in a flash.

Freedom does not lie in possessing the object of desire.
Nor does it lie on the other side of desire,
for that would also create separation and attachment.
We would become prisoners of our desire to be free.

Freedom lies in awareness and acceptance
of everything just as it is.
No separation. No attachments. No obstacles.
Nothing between you and what is.

Just dwelling in awareness and acceptance.
Your actions arising in natural harmony with what is.
Being here now and letting everything else go.
This is freedom from desire.
This is freedom.

The *Tao Te Ching* makes many mentions of desire as something standing between us and peace. For example, "When there is no desire, all things are at peace" (chapter 37). Similarly, "If you close your mind in judgments and traffic with desires, your heart will be troubled. If you keep your mind from judging and aren't led by the senses, your heart will find peace" (chapter 52). It seems desire is the root of much trouble and confusion. This observation explores how desire works. If we are aware of how it works, then perhaps we can nip desire in the bud and thereby experience more peace in our lives.

The observation starts with a simple case: desiring an object you want to possess. This is simple because it is typically obvious what the object is, and whether or not it's "yours" is easy to determine. A fancy car is a good enough example. When you desire the car, here is what happens: you immediately become trapped by two forces, both of which you have created.

The first is separation and the second is attachment. You are obviously separated from possessing the car because you do not possess it yet. And what you are attached to is the idea of possessing it sometime in the future. The trouble is that separation and peace of mind do not go together. And the trouble is about to get worse because your actions will now be driven by desire. "Thus, to the degree you desire, you are both separated and attached. You are no longer free." The observation suggests there is only one place where freedom lies, and that is in accepting the world "just as it is."

But if we don't do anything to get the car, then how will it ever be ours? This is a good question. And the answer lies in understanding that acceptance is not the same as doing nothing. Accepting the world as it is does not mean you do nothing. Nor does it mean that if you do something you will necessarily end up possessing the car. Maybe you will possess it, maybe you won't. However, in the meantime, what is certain is that if you accept the world "as it is" you will be free of desire—car or no car. This freedom is what brings peace of mind and allows your actions to flow without effort. "The Master's power is like this. He lets things come and go effortlessly, without desire" (chapter 55).

A less simple case is to desire a state of being rather than an object—for example, a state of happiness or peace or even simply a state of being free from desire. But this observation points out that desire always causes separation and attachment to come into play—every time. It does not matter whether it is an object or a state of being. With respect to the last example, "we would become prisoners of our desire to be free." We would first identify our separation from freedom and then become attached to the idea of having it. Separation and attachment; the same as before. And those would be exactly what would keep us trapped. It seems desire is very difficult to deal with!

The observation continues, "Freedom lies in awareness and acceptance of everything just as it is. No separation. No attachments. No obstacles. Nothing between you and what is." But, we might ask, isn't desire the motivating force behind everything we do? The answer is that it can be if we let it. However, if our actions are driven by desire, then sooner or later, we should expect what the *Tao Te Ching* calls "confusion and sorrow." Alternatively, we can simply act in harmony with the Tao and leave desire out of the picture altogether. And when we do, "people would be content with their simple, everyday lives. In harmony, and free of desire" (chapter 37).

What does living in harmony look like? Here's a good answer: "Therefore the Master takes action by letting things take their course. He remains as calm at the end as at the beginning. He has nothing, thus has nothing to lose. What he desires is non-desire; what he learns is to unlearn" (chapter 64). Thus the Master still acts, but his actions flow in harmony with the Tao—they are not driven by desire. This is the difference. This is why the Master is free and why what he experiences is calmness.

How often we act in response to desire. Rather than accept whatever is here right now, it seems we prefer to imagine a "better" version of reality. We then judge the current version as falling short and get to work to rearrange the world until it matches this "better" version. To do this is to live in separation from what is and in attachment to the way we want things to be. Examples include not only material possessions but also money, security, and the esteem of others. "Chase after money and security and your heart will never unclench. Care about people's approval and you will be their prisoner" (chapter 9). Every time we do this we get trapped.

What if, instead of starting from desire, we started from awareness and acceptance? If we did, we would not see our actions as tools for rearranging the world. Instead, our actions would be responses "arising in natural harmony with what is."

This chapter's observation reminds us that this is what freedom from desire looks like. What's more, it suggests that this is what freedom actually is.

13
MUSIC

We can make music take many forms.
Music in words is poetry.
Music in motion is dance.
Music in life is love.
At least, so say I.

Music and love are both gifts.
As they have been given,
there's no need to try to make them.
We need only to share them.

We can only try to make sense,
as we cannot take sense for granted.
The point is, we don't need to succeed
in order to understand.

If what I have written doesn't make sense,
then don't try to understand it.
Just listen to the music.

All I have tried to do
is share what I hear.

This observation looks at how dwelling in the Tao is all about responding to the harmony. We can best respond to something only once we are aware of it. So, to first hear harmony, "empty your mind of all thoughts. Let your heart be at peace" (chapter 16). To empty our mind of thoughts is to let go of the endless chatter inside our head. Only then can we hear the harmony that is there all the time. This observation refers to the harmony as "music."

Once we can hear the music, we can respond to it in many ways. We can literally make music by creating harmony between musical notes when we sing or play musical instruments. But there are also many types of metaphorical music, and we give them various names. There is music in the patterns between words, which we call poetry. There is music in the arrangement of color on an artist's canvas. There is music in the flow of a dancer's movements. And there can also be music in the flow of what we do as we live our human lives. This observation suggests, "Music in life is love."

The observation then invites us to think of our role as not so much to make the music itself as simply to find forms for expressing it. It suggests the music is a given, as it were; it is already there. It is not something we create out of nothing. "Music and love are both gifts." Our role is simply to find ways to express them and share them.

However, there is one thing that is not already there, and that is what we call sense. And sense seems to fascinate us. We like to make sense of things. However, sense is definitely not a given. So, if we want sense, then indeed we do have to make it. "We can only try to make sense, as we cannot take sense for granted." And if you look at what we choose to do with our time, it seems we spend a lot of time making sense—or at least trying to.

Why do we do this? I think it is because we think that making sense of something is the way to understand it. Our way of doing this is to build what we call "knowledge" about it. So we analyze what we perceive as being "out there." And the way we analyze something is with thought. We identify something and then separate it into parts, which we name, organize, and put back together again into various structures we call knowledge. "In the pursuit of knowledge, every day something is added" (chapter 48). This is how we build knowledge and make what we call "sense" of things. And it can be a useful exercise with many practical applications.

But the trouble is that this type of knowledge is not the same as understanding. The *Tao Te Ching* draws a sharp distinction between them. "The more you know, the less you understand" (chapter 47). While there is nothing wrong with knowledge, it is simply not required for living in harmony with the Tao. What's more, if we are not careful, knowledge tends to get in the way. This is why "in the practice of the Tao, every day something is dropped" (chapter 48). We are welcome to try to make sense if we want to but, as this observation says, "the point is, we don't need to succeed in order to understand."

So, if understanding does not lie in making sense, then where does it lie? The answer is, it lies in the music. In the case of words, the music lies not in the words themselves but in what they point to. This is why writers write. This is why readers read. Do the words make sense? Maybe they do, maybe they don't. It really doesn't matter. All that matters is whether the reader can hear the music. If the words get in the way, then forget trying to make sense of them—just listen to the music. For example, if you can hear the music right now as you are reading, then this observation has succeeded. That is all these written words are trying to do. They have no other purpose.

How often we try to make sense of things. How often we like to accumulate knowledge. While certainly useful in many ways, knowledge can also be a great distraction. It can be the source of endless discussion, endless questions, endless seeking. In fact, if we are not careful, the "pursuit of knowledge" can consume much of the time in our lives.

What if the music is there all the time, right beneath our feet, as it were? What if it is not something we need to pursue? What if the music is not so much something we build knowledge about as simply listen to and respond to? What if, when we respond, we become part of the harmony? That would be worth exploring, wouldn't it?

This chapter's observation reminds us that music and love are both gifts. All we need to do is accept them and make them into various forms for sharing.

14
THOUGHTS AND DREAMS

I am not my thoughts. I am not my feelings.
I am a droplet of self-consciousness
in the vast flow of everything that is.
With self-consciousness comes choice.
I can be part of the flow or push against it.

To be part of the flow is to listen to the universe
and become aware of my unique part in helping it unfold.
Acting with compassion and letting go.
Trusting the flow.

To push against the flow is to be unaware of it.
Acting as if there is no flow or not trusting it.
Standing separate and apart,
attempting to direct and control.

With the first come joy, peace, and serenity.
With the second come various forms of confusion and sorrow.
Yet the second is nothing more than a dream
from which we can wake any time we choose.
The dream is self-consciousness.

We sleep when we focus on ourselves.
We dream every time we try to stand separate and apart,
when we think that my thoughts are different from yours,
my feelings are different from yours,
that I am different from you,
and we are different from the vast flow.

But the moment we recall that we are not our thoughts,
that we are not our feelings, the difference disappears.
Self-consciousness evaporates.
The dream vanishes. We wake up.
We become aware there are no differences.
There is no separation. Only unity.
And the droplet has dissolved
in the vast flow of everything that is.

This observation explores self-consciousness. There is no doubt that during this human life we experience what we call our self. But there is always the question, Who exactly are we? How can we know we exist? These are classic philosophical questions and there are classic philosophical answers. Many of the answers are quite complicated and involve specialized terminology. This observation takes a simple approach.

It seems one thing we can be certain of is that we have thoughts and feelings. Descartes famously identified awareness of thought as the proof of existence when he wrote, "I think, therefore I am." True though this may be, however, the thinker is not the same thing as the thought. Nor is this true of feelings. Hence the opening line of this observation, "I am not my thoughts. I am not my feelings." So if we are neither of these, then who are we? For all practical, everyday purposes, we see ourselves as a "self" that is capable of having thoughts and feelings. In other words, who we think we are is our self. This is what we are conscious of, which is why we describe ourselves as "self-conscious."

To be self-conscious is, therefore, to see oneself as separate and apart from everything else. We appear to be here, the world appears to be out there, and we experience this state of affairs for the length of a human lifetime. For this brief time span, we get to be a droplet of self-consciousness, as it were, "in the vast flow of everything that is." The question is, What do we do with our human life? This observation suggests we have two choices. We can be part of the flow or we can push against it.

To be part of the flow is to be aware of it and to trust it. When we do this, we start by listening to the flow and discovering that not only is it vastly bigger than we are, it is also continuously unfolding. We can then contribute to the unfolding going on around us, which is so much bigger than ourselves. This observation simply calls it "the universe." When we contribute in this way, we respond to where the universe is coming from, as it were. "Acting with compassion and letting go." (Compassion simply means we do not put our self first.) This is how the Master responds. "Things arise and she lets them come;

things disappear and she lets them go. She has but doesn't possess, acts but doesn't expect" (chapter 2). And when we do this, something interesting happens. We experience joy, peace, and serenity.

However, we can also act as if the flow does not exist. We can do this in a couple of ways. We can either be unaware of the flow or, if we are aware of it, we can decide not to trust it. Either way, to do this is to keep ourselves separate and apart. We see our role as to direct and control a stream of events to suit ourselves, regardless of where they are coming from. This is to put our self first. Whenever we do so, we have expectations in mind. In this, we immediately become unlike the Master, who "acts but doesn't expect." When we act to fulfill our expectations, we push against the flow. And when we do this, something else interesting happens. What we often experience is stress, confusion, and sorrow.

There is an obvious question. Why would we do anything other than respond to the flow? Why would we pick stress, confusion, and sorrow when we could pick joy, peace, and serenity? I think the answer lies in how we view our self. Given what is at stake, this is well worth exploring.

Are we really separate and apart, and is the world simply a playground for satisfying our desires until our life is over? This observation suggests that to think so is to live and act as if we are in a dream. In contrast, to be awake is to be aware that self-consciousness is an illusion. The Master "dwells in reality, and lets all illusions go" (chapter 38). To be awake is to be aware that the only eternal reality is the Oneness/Wholeness that is everything. It even includes the illusion that we are separate and apart.

From inside our human lives, self-consciousness certainly appears real. But this observation suggests that to live as though it is the only reality is to remain asleep, to dream, and to live in the illusion. So, how do we wake up? The answer is simply to be aware that we are not our thoughts, and we are not our feelings. We are not even the self that is having the thoughts and feelings. To be awake is to be aware that "there is no separation. Only unity." Once awake, we realize that who we are is already part of this Oneness/Wholeness. The Master realizes this. He does not see himself as separate. "He doesn't think about his actions;

they flow from the core of his being" (chapter 50). You could even say he "has dissolved in the vast flow of everything that is."

How often we live inside the dream. The illusion is a powerful one. How do we know it is not real? What is the proof that it is not real? Who am I to say I am awake and you are asleep, or vice versa for that matter? I think the answer lies in our experience of life.

Have you ever felt as if your life was an endless struggle to satisfy your desires? At other times, have you felt as if your actions flowed effortlessly "from the core of your being"? I think that when we experience struggle, it is a clue that we are living inside the dream. When we accept reality just as it is and seem able to contribute to the flow of everything around us without effort and without expectation, it is a clue that we are awake. When we are awake, we do not even think about it. To think about it is to fall asleep again.

This chapter's observation reminds us that waking up is a choice. And it is a choice we need to keep making if we are to stay awake.

15
ON THE OTHER SIDE

On the other side of thought we stop making distinctions.
No shades of meaning. No words. No noise.
Just emptiness and silence.

Then we discover that instead of shade there is light.
Instead of silence there is harmony.
And we become aware they are there all the time,
on both sides of thought.

It's just that on this side it is too dark and noisy
to see and hear them.
On the other side there is nothing in the way.

Just light and harmony
with no distinction between them.

Most of the time we live in a world of thoughts. We like to analyze things, separate them into parts, and name them. Thought is all about making distinctions between things. After all, if we cannot separate and distinguish things from one another, then how can we think about them and talk about them? The more we analyze, the more subtle our distinctions become. We talk about meaning and discuss subtle differences between shades of meaning. The world of thoughts is very full of things. It is also full of shades—and shade suggests darkness.

Clearly, we desire to understand everything in terms we can think and talk about. However, the *Tao Te Ching* suggests these terms are no more than artifacts of our minds. "The tao that can be told is not the eternal Tao. The name that can be named is not the eternal Name. The unnamable is the eternally real. Naming is the origin of all particular things" (chapter 1). This means that whatever we can name and talk about is never the eternally real; it is always simply a "manifestation" of the eternally real. And there are literally as many manifestations as we can think of.

As far as our minds are concerned, the eternally real remains a mystery. Not only can we never talk about it, it also remains something we can never realize. The only way we can realize it is to recognize that desire is a trap, as it were, and to let go of it. "Free from desire, you realize the mystery. Caught in desire, you see only the manifestations" (chapter 1). To be caught in desire is to remain on this side of thought. This observation asks the question, What is on the other side and how do we get there?

On the other side is eternal reality. But when we look at it from the world of thought, we cannot see it. We see no familiar shades of meaning, not even any differences between things. In fact, we cannot see any "things." Eternal reality may be the source of everything, but, as far as we can see, it is all dark. "Mystery and manifestations arise from the same source. The source is called darkness. Darkness within darkness. The gateway to all understanding" (chapter 1). The only way to go through the gateway is to let go of thought and come out on the other side. "Empty your mind of all thoughts. Let your heart be at peace" (chapter 16).

When we do this, we make a surprising discovery. On the other side of the gateway it is not dark after all. It is light. Everywhere. Instead of the constant chatter of our own thoughts, at first there is silence. Then, when we listen, we can hear harmony. Everywhere. "And we become aware they are there all the time, on both sides of thought." So, why can we not see them all the time?

The answer is because, most of the time, we live on this side of the gateway. Our world of thoughts is full of shades of meaning, with darkness between the shadows. What's more, it is also a world full of noise as different thoughts clamor for our attention. Thought is exactly what gets in the way of seeing the light and the harmony. "On the other side there is nothing in the way." In eternal reality there are no distinctions between anything because there are no "things." Eternal reality is just Oneness/Wholeness.

In fact, when you think about it, even to talk about light and harmony is to give them names like "light" and "harmony" and thereby make distinctions between them. This is exactly what happens when you think about things—distinctions appear. And so the observation ends by letting us know that light and harmony are there all the time but, then again, not really—because at the level of Oneness/Wholeness there is no distinction between them.

How comfortable we feel in our world of thoughts. We share thoughts with others, talk about them, and discuss them. It is a familiar world. Does it matter that none of it is "eternally real" and that the things we talk about are no more than "manifestations"? To a certain extent, no, it does not matter. It starts to matter only if we believe that what we can see and talk about is all there is, and if the only thing we take direction from is our own thoughts.

Have you ever emptied "your mind of all thoughts"? What happened when you did that? What did you see and hear? Of course, that's not a fair question because the answer will not be anything you can describe in words! If we were both on this side of the gateway, you might use words like "light" and "harmony." But on the other side, as we have seen, words do not work anymore. There is simply awareness. If we were both on the other side of the gateway, then all we could do is smile at each other. There would be no need to do anything else. Besides, there would be nothing to say. And, for that matter, the concept of "each other" would have disappeared as well.

This chapter's observation reminds us that our world of thoughts may be familiar, but it is noisy and distracting. When we become aware that what we can see and talk about is not all there is, we begin to let go of taking direction from nothing but thought. To do this is to come out from the shadows and into the light, to leave behind the noise and hear the harmony—to go through the gateway.

We can tell when we are out on the other side of the gateway because distinctions between light and harmony disappear. There will be only Oneness/Wholeness. And we will realize it was there all along. That is enough to make you smile.

16
INSIDE THE BOX

Thought has its place as we move in this world.
There are groceries to buy, cars to be fixed,
airports where we have to arrive on time.
Thought can do a great job of managing this worldly business.
But that's where its business ends.
The world is like a box and thought belongs inside it.

Trouble comes when thought takes on a life of its own.
Sometimes it climbs outside the box, puffs itself up,
beats its chest, and lays claim to all it can see.
No longer servant, it acts like master.
And we often let it get away with doing so.
After all, it does a good job with the grocery list.
Perhaps we should trust it with everything else.

But here's what happens. Give it a chance
and thought will no longer serve you—it will serve itself.
Puffed up, with a life of its own, it is none other than your ego.
Getting to the airport on time is easy. Grocery lists are trivial.
Much more interesting is to calculate
the future return on investment for various actions.

How best to satisfy desires?
How best to accumulate possessions?
How best to impress others?
And when you act in response, your roles reverse.
You become the servant and your ego is master.

So remember, the world is like a box and thought belongs inside it.
Be on guard for when it tries to get out.
Ensure that it remains your servant and not your master.
Live as much as you can where it matters most, outside the box.
But keep thought in its place:
inside the box.

There is something very down-to-earth about living in this world. If nothing else, our human bodies require care and attention—it seems they do not look after themselves. At the very least, they require food and water and sleep. Whether we like it or not, our active involvement is required. This is also true for many other practical aspects of day-to-day living. As this observation says, "There are groceries to buy, cars to be fixed, and airports where we have to arrive on time."

Early on in our lives we learn that whenever it is going to take more than one step to get something done, it's a good idea to think about it before we start. If we don't, then we learn by trial and error that there are many ways to waste time and effort. So, unless we enjoy the trial-and-error process itself, we learn not only what we need to do but also how to plan and get the result we want as efficiently as possible.

This is where thought comes in. And thought is the perfect tool for the job. While it's always good to use the right tool, when the job is done, it is also best to put the tool right back where it belongs—in the toolbox. This observation looks at what happens when we forget to do that.

What happens is that we get trouble. Perhaps the images are bit colorful. Does thought really "take on a life of its own"? Does it really climb outside the box, puff itself up, beat its chest, and lay claim to all it can see? The answer is no, not unless we let it. The trouble is, we often do. "After all, it does a good job with the grocery list. Perhaps we should trust it with everything else." But, as soon as we let that happen, thought is no longer a tool—it starts to run the show. "No longer servant, it acts like master."

When thought acts like a master it considers questions like "How best to satisfy desires? How best to accumulate possessions? How best to impress others?" Left unchecked, thought will then come up with its own answers to these questions. And it does not stop there. Thought will then, as it were, direct you to take the necessary actions to make the answers a reality—or at least to try to. But wait a minute. Who is doing this thinking? This is not the real you. If you want to give it a name, you could call it your ego. When you live your life driven by your ego, you will never know peace and serenity. There will always be trouble of one sort or another.

The *Tao Te Ching* makes this quite clear. "When there is no desire, all things are at peace" (chapter 37). "If you overvalue possessions, people begin to steal" (chapter 3). "Other people have what they need; I alone possess nothing" (chapter 20). "Chase after money and security and your heart will never unclench. Care about people's approval and you will be their prisoner" (chapter 9). Stealing, chasing, being a prisoner. . . . Doesn't sound like peace and serenity, does it?

Regardless of what our ego thinks, living in harmony with the world around us is not about satisfying desires, chasing after possessions, and putting ourselves at the center of everything we do. Let us look at what the Master does. "The Master has no possessions. The more he does for others, the happier he is. The more he gives to others, the wealthier he is" (chapter 81). What does that mean to us? In short, it means we should ensure that thought remains our servant and not our master. It means we should pick up thought like a useful tool when there is a need for it, and then put it carefully back in the box when we are done. "Keep thought in its place. Inside the box."

How often we let thought run the show. How often we let our egos direct our actions. You would think that after repeatedly experiencing the confusion and stress this approach creates, we would learn through trial and error. Not so, apparently. We seem capable of experiencing many "errors" without learning that we often cause them for ourselves. Perhaps part of the problem comes from the well-known saying "think outside the box," which is always said as though it is a good thing to do. Maybe we should think twice about that!

What if we paused before reaching into the toolbox? What if we asked ourselves: Is this a puzzle or problem or situation for which thought is the best tool for finding a solution? I think we would be surprised at how often the answer would be no. And then, putting thought aside, we would be free to accept how the world is unfolding and simply respond by contributing to it the same way the Master does: "He doesn't think about his actions; they flow from the core of his being" (chapter 50).

This chapter's observation reminds us that much of living does not require reaching into the toolbox. If we decide to reach in, then we should do so carefully. And, when we are done, we should also be careful to put the tools back where they belong. When we do both those things, I think we are much more likely to experience peace and harmony.

17
TEACHERS AND FRIENDS

No one can teach you, but you can learn from others.
No one can take you anywhere, but someone can point the way.
No one can travel your journey for you,
but someone can keep you company
as you travel on your path,
even as they travel on theirs.

You learn only when you are ready.
You follow your own path only when you can see or can trust.
But someone may point to the path
or happen to be present when you learn.
This person is a teacher.

You travel only as you move your own feet forward.
But someone can be beside you
and catch you if you stumble,
or help you get up if you fall.
This person is a friend.

Friends can be teachers.
Teachers can be friends.
They are on their own paths,
yet their company is one of the greatest joys in life.
And you too can be that joy in a fellow traveler's life.

All you need do is always be open to receiving.
Always be open to giving.
Always be open.
Always.

To learn is to change some aspect of how you respond to life. Everything you do is a response, and all responses produce outcomes of one sort or another. When you do something that produces an outcome you don't like and you later recognize a similar situation coming along, then you simply don't do the same thing again. We call that learning. In this case, you learn from your own direct experience. We sometimes call it learning from your mistakes. (Although the word "mistake" adds little value.) However, there are also other ways to learn.

Other people can deliberately show you things without your having to experience them directly for yourself. We call these people teachers. And you can also learn about things that are more abstract, such as the subjects typically taught in school, like mathematics, history, art, music, languages, and literature. Schools and teachers can help create the best conditions for learning to take place but, in the end, you are always the one doing the learning.

Sometimes we confuse the process with the result. We think that because you are in school, being taught formal lessons, being exposed to books full of words and knowledge, you must be learning something. But the result is that maybe you are, or maybe you aren't. The best teachers know it's not about them and what they do; it is about you. "Teaching without words, performing without actions: that is the Master's way" (chapter 43). In fact, the best teaching requires no words at all. "The Master, by residing in the Tao, sets an example for all beings" (chapter 22). And she knows what she is doing. "Thus the Master is content to serve as an example and not to impose her will" (chapter 58).

We sometimes describe life as being like a journey, in which case what we learn from others can help us along the way. But just as we each learn for ourselves, we are each on our own path and we travel it for ourselves. Our journey is ours and no one else's. This observation explores what happens when we meet certain people on our journey. These people are teachers and friends.

Teachers cannot travel our path for us, but they can point the way. They may do so deliberately in school, or they may do so in other ways. What's more, we may recognize what is going on when it happens and be aware that we are learning from them, or we may be unaware. "The

Master doesn't talk, he acts. When his work is done, the people say, 'Amazing: we did it, all by ourselves!'" (chapter 17). In this case, the people are clearly unaware. But the point is, it really does not matter how the learning takes place, or whether or not we are aware of it. A teacher is simply someone from whom we learn.

Similarly, as we all know, traveling along the path of our life is not always easy going. Sometimes it is difficult; sometimes very difficult indeed. But we are not alone. We can always reach out and help one another. In the words of this observation, "Someone can be beside you to catch you if you stumble, or help you get up if you fall. This person is a friend."

In fact, the best friends point out things that can help us even when we do not seem to have fallen yet. Sometimes we are not ready to hear what they have to say, especially if we interpret their words as criticism. But if a person is ready to listen and learn, then "he considers those who point out his faults as his most benevolent teachers" (chapter 61). And it can work in several ways. "Friends can be teachers. Teachers can be friends." And you yourself can be either, or both, to other people. Discovering this is "one of the greatest joys in life." There are only two requirements, and both of them involve being open. The first is to "always be open to receiving." The second requirement is to "always be open to giving." That is all we need to do. It is not complicated.

How often we travel alone. We seem convinced that because no one has traveled our unique path, we have nothing to learn from anyone. What's more, we may believe no one can help us along our way. But we forget that we always see the world in terms of what we believe to be true about it. If we are closed, then we see none of the possibilities we would see if we were open. They are invisible to us. From our point of view, such possibilities simply do not exist. So, sadly for us, indeed they do not exist. What we believe becomes our reality.

Have you ever been helped without being conscious of it at the time? Have you ever noticed what happened but only later, in hindsight? Sometimes it seems we have to learn difficult lessons in life. At such times, depending on the circumstances, we tend not to see the people involved at the time as being our "most benevolent teachers."

If we were not aware of what was taking place, we may even have seen these people as enemies. However, once we are aware, then it becomes clear that how we see the world says more about us than it says about the world. In reality, there are no enemies out there. If an enemy exists, then it lies within. Referring to the Master, the *Tao Te Ching* says, "He thinks of his enemy as the shadow that he himself casts" (chapter 61).

This chapter's observation reminds us that every time we judge, we close our mind. Every time we close our mind, we cannot learn from someone who might have been a teacher. Every time we think we are alone, we cannot accept friendship—nor can we be a friend to someone else. Receiving and giving both require being open. This is neither right nor wrong. It's just the way it is. Always.

18

TURN OFF THE FLASHLIGHT

Thought seems like a flashlight shining in the darkness,
lighting up objects for us to see.
Everywhere we turn the flashlight, separate objects appear.
They glint and sparkle and fascinate.
If we turn off the flashlight, surely
we will be plunged into darkness.

Let's try. Here's how.
Don't look at the lit-up objects.
Look at the flashlight.
Don't try to shine another light on it.
Don't try to do anything with it.
Just look at it.

Do this and the flashlight will stop shining.
The objects will disappear. The flashlight will disappear.
And all of a sudden you will be plunged into brightness.

No longer does a beam of light distinguish separate things
in separate places, one at a time.
Instead there is brightness everywhere,
illuminating everything all at once.

Nothing is separate any more. There are no shadows.
Everything is brilliant in its Oneness/Wholeness.
And you become aware this is the way it always was
until the moment you turned on the flashlight.

The flashlight is born of your desire to see.
But all you see is the illusion of countless separate things.
So let go of desire. To dwell in the light,
just turn off the flashlight.

The phrases we use every day say a lot about how we see the world. For example, we talk about seeing things more clearly "in the light of day." We say we feel "left in the dark" on some subject. We talk about clarifying a situation by "shedding light" on it. It seems we associate darkness with not understanding something, and we like to understand things—or at least we like to think we do.

This observation uses the image of a flashlight to illustrate how thought works. When we shine a light on something we can see it for what it is. (Strictly speaking, we see it for what we think it is.) If we have seen it before, we may recognize it. It likely has a name by which we can distinguish it from everything else. Over the centuries we have developed conventions for how we name things. This allows us to talk about things to other people, who will know what we're talking about. It's all very organized.

The pursuit of knowledge is also fascinating. It seems "everywhere we turn the flashlight separate objects appear. They glint and sparkle and fascinate." The world appears to be populated with thousands of separate things. We can spend hours, days, and even a whole lifetime sifting, sorting, and organizing pieces of knowledge. As the *Tao Te Ching* reminds us, "In the pursuit of knowledge, every day something is added" (chapter 48).

The trouble is, we can become so attached to our flashlight that we believe it is the only way to see anything. This means when we cannot see anything, we typically think nothing is there—and we associate nothing with darkness. This is why we trust our flashlight. "If we turn off the flashlight, surely we will be plunged into darkness." At least, that is what we think. Let's try it and see. But how exactly do we turn off the flashlight?

This observation suggests that one way to do this is to look at how we light things up rather than at what we think we see as a result. In other words, to look directly at the flashlight itself rather than whatever we are pointing it at. This is not something we are used to doing. In fact, we will likely find it quite difficult. But when we succeed, something surprising happens.

From our point of view, objects disappear when we are no longer looking at them. But interestingly, this also applies to the flashlight itself. The flashlight cannot light itself up, as it were, because it is the thing doing the lighting. This means when we look directly at the flashlight, we cannot see it because the flashlight itself is in the dark. And so is everything else the flashlight is not shining at. In the darkness, we cannot see anything. And then comes the surprise. The moment we stop thinking about what we can and cannot see, suddenly there is brightness everywhere. All on its own. And we discover that the brightness has nothing to do with the flashlight; it also has nothing to do with us. The brightness is simply there.

What do we see? Clearly, we see nothing we can separate out and name. Instead, what we see is the Oneness/Wholeness of everything, everywhere, all at once. What is this? Here is an attempt to describe it: "There was something formless and perfect before the universe was born. It is serene. Empty. Solitary. Unchanging. Infinite. Eternally present. It is the mother of the universe. For lack of a better name, I call it the Tao" (chapter 25).

The Tao is there all the time. It is there when the flashlight is turned on, and it is there when the flashlight is turned off. The only difference is that when the flashlight is turned on, we cannot see it. Instead, we see "the illusion of countless separate things." The *Tao Te Ching* is quite clear that this is not where reality lies. This is why the Master dwells in the Tao. "He dwells in reality, and lets all illusions go" (chapter 38). This observation suggests, "The flashlight is born of your desire to see." So the way to turn it off is simply to "let go of desire."

How often we seem to trust only what we can see. We believe the way to understand the whole is to shine a bright light at it, identify as many parts as possible, give them all names, and then assemble them together again. Yet we also have a saying that "the whole is more than the sum of the parts." So, what have we failed to understand? What have we lost with this approach? What we have gained is the merely sum of the parts. What we have lost is the whole.

What if the whole is simply what it is, regardless of whether or not we understand it? What if it has nothing to do with how many parts we think it is made up of? We may feel this would be like living in the dark. But what if living in harmony with something we don't happen to understand turns out to be living in the light? Wouldn't that be worth finding out?

This chapter's observation reminds us that the light is not at the end of a long, dark tunnel. The light is right here, right now if only we would stop looking for it somewhere else. To turn off the flashlight, all we need do is stop looking at things and trying to understand them. Instead, we simply let go and trust what we become aware of.

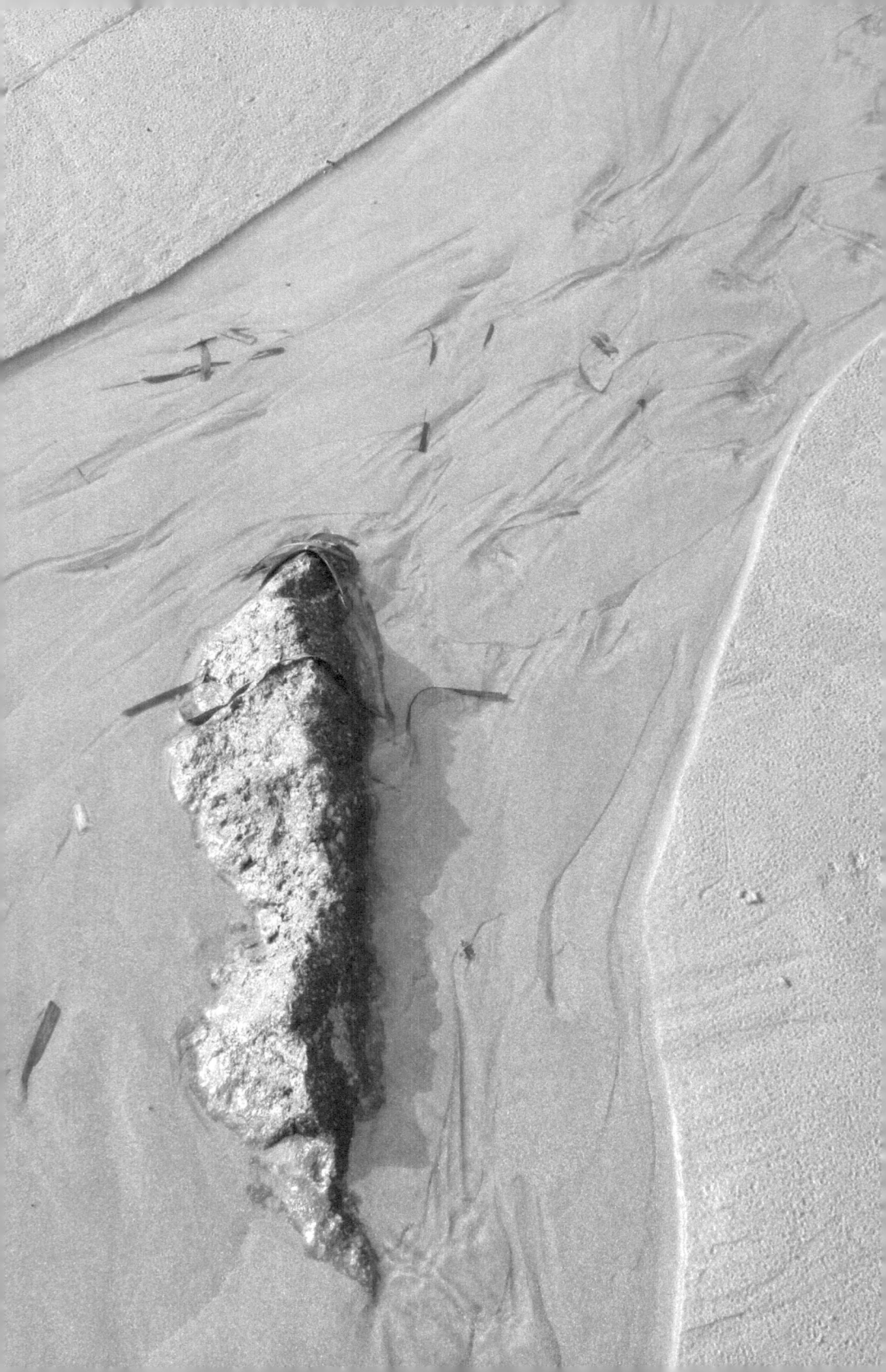

19
INTENTION

To act deliberately is to launch an intention
out into the flow of the unfolding universe.
Your action seems so small and the universe so big,
and its flow is so vast and immense.
Obstacles, undercurrents, rapids,
waterfalls, wind, rain.
So many things over which you have no control.
What difference will your action make?

You can never know for certain,
because the results are not yours to control.
But you have complete control over your intention.
Your actions are yours and yours alone.
Aim to bring light and create harmony.
Then launch your intention
carefully but with confidence.

Be sure to let it go out into the flow on its own.
Do not linger, trying to tinker and adjust.
All you can do is take good care of your intention.
The results will take care of themselves.

Launch your intention.
Step back.
Let go.

Whenever we act, we produce an outcome of one sort or another. Sometimes we have a particular outcome in mind and we get what we want. On the other hand, sometimes things turn out differently. Sometimes they turn out just a little differently; sometimes, a lot. At other times we discover our actions have unintended side effects that we never anticipated at all. We never saw them coming, as we like to say. But we act nonetheless, and we learn early on in our lives that there is a limit to what we can control. This observation explores what is ours to control and what is not—and what we can do about it.

Thinking we can control all the details is what the *Tao Te Ching* refers to as "trying to dominate events." "The Master does his job and then stops. He understands that the universe is forever out of control, and that trying to dominate events goes against the current of the Tao" (chapter 30). However, there is a lot we can do that stops short of trying to dominate events. (As for "the universe is forever out of control," I think the implication is that it is only out of *our* control.) So, if we cannot dominate events, then what is it that we can do? The short answer is that we can act deliberately and then let go. Let's dig a little deeper.

To act deliberately is to have some outcome in mind. We have an intention to make some kind of difference in the world. But before we act, we often wonder how likely we are to succeed. When we think of everything that might get in the way, we can begin to feel that the odds are against us. In the words of this observation, "Your action seems so small and the universe so big, and its flow is so vast and immense. Obstacles, undercurrents, rapids, waterfalls, wind, rain. So many things over which you have no control." It is enough to make you want to give up. But to do so would be to lose sight of the one thing over which you have total control—and that is your intention. What you intend, and what actually happens as a result of what you do, are two separate things. The second may have little to do with the first, except that it follows it.

The first involves answering the question, What is the difference you want to make in the world? What do you intend to bring about as a result of your actions? The more clearly you can answer this question, the clearer your intention becomes. A clear intention is the one thing you can control, and the one thing that gives you the best chance of bringing about the difference you have in mind.

It is worth noting that clarity and detail are not the same. In fact, to have too detailed an intention is to set yourself up for disappointment and frustration when the details fail to turn out exactly the way you want. For this reason, not only are general intentions quite good enough; I think they are often actually better. As this observation says, "Aim to create light and bring harmony." This is about as general as you can get.

If a clear intention is your first step, then your second step is to launch your intention out into "the current of the Tao" by acting on it. And your third and final step is to let it go. What makes the second step hard is worrying about the odds of success. What makes the third step hard is accepting there is only so much we can do. The *Tao Te Ching* reminds us, "Do your work, then step back. The only path to serenity" (chapter 9). "If you want to accord with the Tao, just do your job, then let go" (chapter 24). What we need to accept is that only intention and action are ours to control; the outcome is not. The outcome will always be what it is going to be.

How easy it is to say this. How hard it is to do. Why? I think part of the reason is that we let intention slide into expectation. When we have an outcome in mind, we do not merely intend for it to happen—we expect it to happen. Expectation is what causes the trouble. The Master is aware of this: "Acting with no expectations, leading and not trying to control: this is the supreme virtue" (chapter 10). To let go is to have no expectations. Intention precedes action. Expectation follows it. Expectation is the part we need to let go of. At least, that's the way it seems to me.

How often we act with no particular intention in mind. Much of the time we do not even act so much as react to whatever we feel is happening to us. If you think about it, to react is to give our action no thought at all. In this case, intention does not even get a chance. At other times, we act with intention but we do not let go. Instead, we stay close by in case our actions do not bring about exactly the detailed results we want.

What if we accept that to let go is to trust the outcome regardless of what it is? After all, the outcome is going to be what it's going to be anyway. Why not trust it? What would we rather trust? Would we rather trust our ability to get the results of our actions back on track if it looks like things are not turning out the way we want? What if our role is "creating without possessing, acting without expecting, guiding without interfering" (chapter 51)? This is what the Master does. This is what trust looks like when it is in action.

This chapter's observation reminds us, "Launch your intention. Step back. Let go."

20
EXPERIENCE AND REALITY

There is only one reality.
But, most of the time, we each have our own experience of it.
Your experience is different from mine,
even if we are in the same place at the same time.

When this happens, we do not experience reality as it is.
We experience it in terms of what we expect it to be.
We think it "should" be this or we "would like" it to be that.
Our expectations become the lens through which we see.

Thus what we see is no longer reality
but the gap between reality and our expectation.
What we experience are the gaps.

We have different experiences of the same reality
because your expectations are different from mine,
so your gaps are different from mine.
But it does not have to be this way.

We can also experience reality just as it is.
All we need do is let go of expectation.
When we do this, the lenses disappear,
the gaps disappear—in fact all differences disappear.
Only reality remains.

When this happens, experience and reality become one
      and the same.

What you experience is the same as what I experience.
We both experience reality just as it is.

Harmony is revealed.
It was there all along.

Why do you and I sometimes have different experiences of the same reality? One explanation could be that there are several different realities in existence at the same time. You are experiencing one of them, and I happen to be experiencing another. A simpler explanation would be that there is only one reality, and the reason we are having different experiences of it has something to do with us. This observation suggests the difference lies in us and our expectations.

The *Tao Te Ching* makes quite a few mentions of expectations. Most often they are in connection with the Master. For example, "The Master's power is like this. He lets all things come and go effortlessly, without desire. He never expects results; thus he is never disappointed. He is never disappointed; thus his spirit never grows old" (chapter 55). Staying young in spirit, not being disappointed, and being able to let things come and go effortlessly are all rewards, as it were, of not having expectations. However, this observation explores how expectations do more than simply get in the way of these rewards. It looks at how expectations distort everything we see and experience.

We start by taking a big step backwards. If we are both in the same place at the same time, can we ever have the same experience of the same reality? Yes, I think we can. If we both have nothing in particular on our minds, and we are both enjoying looking at the same sunset, then chances are our experiences are pretty much the same. But in many other instances, this is not the case. Why might this be?

This observation suggests that "we do not experience reality as it is. We experience it in terms of what we expect it to be." If you like, there is reality, and then there is what we expect it to be. And when the two are not the same, there is a gap. "Thus what we see is no longer reality but the gap between reality and our expectations. What we experience are the gaps." We live in the gaps, as it were. The reason we both see the same sunset is that neither of us has an expectation for it to be anything other than what it is. We have no other idea in mind. It is when we live in the gaps that we lose touch with reality and live inside an illusion.

Where do the gaps come from? I think the gaps are determined completely by what we have in mind. In fact, the size of the gap is determined by the extent to which we are expecting anything different from what is actually happening in any given moment. After all, if we changed our mind, the gaps could disappear in an instant. But typically, we do not change our mind. Instead, we think reality is the way we see it. This is why you and I can have different experiences of the same reality. We simply have different things in mind, and we see reality in terms of them. As a result, we may be in the presence of the same reality but "see" and experience different gaps.

Does this matter? I think it depends on what hangs on the differences. Sometimes it doesn't matter, but at other times it does. It matters the moment we start to have opinions about the gaps, especially if we start to judge them as good or bad or right or wrong. When this happens, harmony is lost and conflict is often just around the corner. It also matters because we seek to have our expectations fulfilled, and so we tend to live in the future rather than in the present moment just as it is. "The Master doesn't seek fulfillment. Not seeking, not expecting, she is present, and can welcome all things" (chapter 15). Note that she can welcome all things because she is fully present rather than somewhere else, in the past or the future.

However, this observation points out that it does not need to be this way. "We can also experience reality just as it is. All we need do is let go of expectation. When we do this . . . experience and reality become one and the same. What you experience is the same as what I experience. We both experience reality just as it is." The *Tao Te Ching* reminds us that "acting with no expectations, leading and not trying to control: this is the supreme virtue" (chapter 10). This is so easy to say, but so hard to do!

How often we live in the gaps. We live suspended between reality and whatever version of it we happen to have in mind. Looking for what we expect to see, we fail to see what is right in front of us. And so each of us dwells in his or her own illusion. No wonder we do not experience the same reality. The Master is aware of this. "He dwells in reality, and lets all illusions go" (chapter 38).

Have you ever noticed that even when our expectations are fulfilled, the satisfaction lasts no longer than it takes for new desires and expectations to spring up and take their place? If we are not careful, we can distract ourselves indefinitely, letting ourselves be pulled this way and that—all the while failing to live fully in the present moment.

This chapter's observation reminds us that when we and others let go of desire and expectation, we and they live in the same reality. What's more, we discover that the harmony we search for is there all the time. It always was. All we have to do is stop looking for it somewhere else and expecting it to be there.

21
TRUE ARTISTS

True artists have mastered themselves.
They know their art does not come from them;
it comes through them.
So they get themselves out of the way.

True artists disappear into their art.
They do not sing; they are the song.
They do not dance; they are the dance.
They do not create music; they are the music.

We can all be true artists.
Each day is a canvas; each action a brush stroke.
We do not perform our actions; we are our actions.
We do not live our lives; we are our lives.

What we think makes no difference.
What others think makes no difference.
Thinking about what others think gets in the way every time.
All that matters is what we do.

We can all be true artists every day of our lives.

Is this an observation about art and artists? Yes and no. It is about what we create as we live our lives. This observation invites us to see our lives as works of art, even if they may not feel like that to us as we live them from day to day. Let's explore this idea.

We tend to think of artists as special people, as somehow different and more creative than the rest of us. Similarly, we may think of art as something special because it is displayed in museums and art galleries, often centuries after it was created. What's more, there are different types of art, including performance art, which vanishes the moment it is performed (unless it is recorded). However, whatever it is, we see art as something of value that an artist creates, on purpose, to share with the rest of the world.

For art to be sharable, it has to stand separate from its creator. If it does not stand alone, as it were, it cannot be shared. After all, the painter is not the painting, the dancer is not the dance, and the singer is not the song. Yet, without the artist, we know that nothing sharable would exist. So, where is the artist at the moment of sharing?

The answer is that he or she personally is no longer there. This observation suggests that artists have disappeared into their creations. Artists are aware their art is not about them; it is about something that comes into being through them. They embody their art; if you like, they become their art. This observation suggests this is what makes them "true artists."

The *Tao Te Ching* makes similar observations about the Master. "The Master, by residing in the Tao, sets an example for all beings" (chapter 22). And he does this by stepping out of the way. "Because he doesn't display himself, people can see his light" (chapter 22). If you reside in your self and are intent on displaying yourself, then what you produce is all about you. It therefore depends on what you have in mind when you act. "The Master keeps her mind always at one with the Tao; that is what gives her her radiance" (chapter 21).

What does this mean for those of us who are not Masters? More important, what does it mean for those of us who are neither painters, nor dancers, nor singers? Surely, artists are people who have mastered their craft. Yes, indeed they are. However, this observation opens with the words "true artists have mastered themselves." Mastering yourself is the key, and that is something we can all do. When you are centered in the Tao, as opposed to centered in your self, then it actually doesn't matter what you do. Everything you do will be an expression of the Tao and will therefore be in harmony with the Tao. That is what self-mastery looks like.

Every day, every one of us has the same twenty-four hours to work with. At the end of the day, every one of us has spent it all on one thing or another. We spend it on what we do. This is true for every one of us. So, what exactly do we do with our actions every day? Where does the time go, and what do we have in mind as we spend it? Are our actions all about us, or do we let the light shine through us the way the Master does? Whether or not we are an "artist" is beside the point. As this observation says, "Each day is a canvas, each action a brush stroke." At the end of the day, we are what we do. "We do not perform our actions; we are our actions. We do not live our lives; we are our lives."

When we are centered in our selves, our actions—and our lives—are about fulfilling our desires. Our actions are not ends in themselves; they are done because of the results we think they will produce. For example, we desire more money or more security or the esteem of others. But, if you think about it, chasing after these is a never-ending game. We will never possess them, nor will we ever have enough of them. Instead, we will be chasing indefinitely. "Care about people's approval and you will be their prisoner" (chapter 9). Hence the words of this observation, "Thinking about what others think gets in the way every time. All that matters is what we do." The light shines only when we step our self out of the way and let the Tao shine through us. This is what true artists do. This observation suggests we can do exactly the same.

How often we use our actions to try to get what we want. Our actions are not ends in themselves; they are a means to getting something else. What's more, we judge them as good or bad, right or wrong. If we're feeling more neutral, we might simply judge them as more or less effective according to how good a job they do of fulfilling whatever desires we had in mind at the time. Either way, it is all about us and what we want. What if we centered ourselves in the Tao? And were then like the Master who "doesn't think about his actions; they flow from the core of his being" (chapter 50). If the Tao is at the core of our being, everything we do will be in harmony with the Tao. It's as simple as that.

We all know what it's like to be present at an amazing artistic performance. It can be a live rock concert, a play on a theater stage, or an orchestra performing classical music. It can also be a picture painted on a canvas or a sculpture carved in stone. It does not matter what it is. Something shines through and we feel the light. What's more, the light is something that comes from beyond time and space; it can come from centuries ago. What was the artist doing when he or she created it? The *Tao Te Ching* calls it "embodying the light" (chapter 27).

This chapter's observation reminds us we can all embody the light every day of our lives. We can all be "true artists."

22
REVEALING THE PATTERN

Your job as an artist is to reveal
a pattern that is already present.
You do this by removing whatever blocks the view.

First, remove everything that blocks the view you see.
Then show the view to others so that,
hopefully, they can see it too.

But stay humble.
Remember, you did not create the pattern.
All you can create are opportunities
for others to see what you see.

The pattern is there all along.
Your job is simply to see it and reveal it.

The previous observation, "True Artists," suggested, "We can all be true artists every day of our lives." As we live our lives, "each day is a canvas, each action a brush stroke." In other words, we can use our actions to make every day into a work of art, as it were. This observation looks at what happens when we use our actions to make something material into a work of art that others can look at—for example, a painting or a sculpture. This is the kind of art that typically springs to mind. Interestingly, there is a similarity between making a material work of art and living our life as though our life is a work of art. This observation explores what this similarity is.

There is a quote attributed to Michelangelo: "I saw the angel inside the marble and carved until I set him free." We may think Michelangelo created the angel, but he says all he did was carve away everything in the marble that was not the angel so that, by the time he was done, only the angel remained. In doing this, to my mind, he did two extraordinary things. He saw the angel in the marble in the first place. Second, he knew exactly how to set him free. Most of us would likely have seen nothing but a block of stone, and we would have had no idea how to set anything free from inside it.

This observation suggests, "Your job as an artist is to reveal a pattern that is already present." Here is the similarity. To do this, you follow the same two steps as Michelangelo. First you see the pattern, then you reveal it. How do you reveal it? "By removing whatever blocks the view." For Michelangelo, what blocked the view was the marble that ended up as chips on his workshop floor. In a more general sense, we can think of what blocks the view as anything that is something other than the view itself.

In both cases, the view is not created—it is revealed. According to Michelangelo, the angel was already there. All he did was see it and then set it free so others could see it too. As this observation notes, "Remember, you did not create the pattern. All you can create are opportunities for others to see what you see." As the saying goes, art makes visible the invisible.

In the *Tao Te Ching*, I think the ultimate "pattern" is the Oneness/Wholeness that is everything. Being beyond words, it cannot be described. Just as a reminder, here is an attempt. "There was something formless and perfect before the universe was born. It is serene. Empty. Solitary. Unchanging. Infinite. Eternally present. It is the mother of the universe. For lack of a better name, I call it the Tao" (chapter 25). "Serene," "empty," "unchanging," and "infinite" are attempts to describe it—and all the words fall short. Hence Lao Tzu concludes, "For lack of a better name, I call it the Tao." Other attempts could include words like "harmony" and "light," which fall short too; but at least they suggest helpful images.

In the current context, to let the light shine is to remove whatever might be blocking it. The *Tao Te Ching* suggests that the light is everywhere, including inside us. The reason we tend not to see it is that we block it with our thoughts and desires. "Can you cleanse your inner vision until you see nothing but the light?" (chapter 10). The light is there all the time. We are the ones who get in the way with our thoughts and desires. The Master knows that if the light does not shine, it is because of "the shadow that he himself casts" (chapter 61). Hence, "the Master, by residing in the Tao, sets an example for all beings. Because he doesn't display himself, people can see his light" (chapter 22).

In short, we do not create the light; it is there all along. Our job is simply to get ourselves out of the way and let it shine. Similarly, Michelangelo did not create the angel; the angel was there all along. He simply carved until he set it free. The result is that we can still see its light shining today—all these centuries later.

How often we fail to see the pattern and the beauty that are already there, right in front of us. How often we fill our moments with the patterns we think should be there and then get to work to bend the world to our wishes. As a result, this is what our "inner vision" becomes full of. This is what blocks the light and causes the endless striving to fulfill our desires.

Whether we strive or not, we can all create things of beauty, or moments of beauty, that both we and others can experience. However, when we succeed, we often go on to hope we are noticed by others. When we do this, we are not so much interested in letting the light shine as in fame and fortune. We associate our work with our self, and we cling to it. It is all about us. But the *Tao Te Ching* reminds us, "He who clings to his work will create nothing that endures" (chapter 24). What's more, "He who tries to shine dims his own light" (chapter 24).

What if we saw our job as simply to create opportunities for the light to shine? If we did that, then it wouldn't be about us; it would be about the light. Instead of striving to bend the world to our wishes, we would ask ourselves questions like the following: Where is the light in this situation? How can I bring light into someone else's life? Can I help dispel clouds of conflict so the light can shine through? Can I reach out to someone who is in darkness? Or, if I am a painter or a sculptor, I would ask: Can I create an opportunity for the light to shine through what I make and leave behind after I die? That is the question Michelangelo answered. His angel shows us the answer was yes.

This chapter's observation reminds us, "The pattern is there all along. Your job is simply to see it and reveal it." Every day brings countless opportunities to do this. And we don't have to be painters or sculptors to do it. We can all create opportunities to let the light shine.

23
BE LIKE WATER

Water does not judge the rock in its path.
It does not even think about it.
It just flows around it.
Be like water.

Always two options.
Option One goes like this:
There is something in my path.
It's a rock. It's a big rock.
Why is this big rock in my path?
This rock should not be there.
It's not what I expected.

What's more . . .
It's a bigger rock than the last rock I remember.
Maybe not. Let's do a rock comparison.
Yes, it's definitely bigger.

What's more . . .
Other people don't have rocks in their paths.
Maybe they do. Let's compare my rock with theirs.
Yes, mine is bigger. I knew it.
It's not fair, not right, not . . .

Option Two goes like this:
A rock? What rock?
Oh, I see it's behind me.

Always two options.
You pick.
Be like water.

We can learn a lot from water. It has no shape of its own; its shape comes from its surroundings. If it's in a lake, then it is lake-shaped. If it's in a pot, then it is pot-shaped. Wherever it is, water puts up no resistance, as it were. This observation invites us, in a humorous way, to learn from water when we encounter what we see as obstacles in our path.

Whenever we embark on a journey, it is natural to hope for good weather and easy travels. Sometimes we get both, and the journey is pleasant and smooth. But sometimes we do not. Perhaps things do not go according to plan, or perhaps we simply find the journey more difficult than we expected. Sometimes it feels like there are obstacles in our path. Maybe the obstacles are even big enough to stop us in our tracks. Whenever this happens, the interesting question is this: How do we respond?

Our response is almost never to welcome the obstacle. After all, we just wanted to fulfill our journey plans. We were not expecting an obstacle. The *Tao Te Ching* reminds us, "The Master doesn't seek fulfillment. Not seeking, not expecting, she is present, and can welcome all things" (chapter 15). How can the Master welcome all things? Part of the answer is that, unlike us, the Master does not stop and judge. Yet, typically, that is exactly what we do. If you think about it, even the word "obstacle" is a judgment because it implies something that is in the way.

This is why water is such a great metaphor. This observation starts, "Water does not judge the rock in its path." Of course, it doesn't. From the water's point of view, as it were, a rock is a rock. It's not an "obstacle," it is just a rock. In fact, it's not even a "rock." If anything, it is simply something that water cannot flow through, so instead the water flows around it. It actually does not matter what it is. It doesn't even need a name. End of story. But, of course, water does not think. However, we do. In fact, we think a lot. And when we think too much, we create problems for ourselves (and often for others). This observation listens in, as it were, on what our thoughts might be. In doing so, it picks up on three levels of unhelpful thinking.

First, we do not simply observe something in our path that we can flow around. Instead, we identify it as a rock, which—oddly enough—we then choose to question. "Why is this big rock in my path?" What's more, we compare its presence with what we expected and boldly pronounce, "This rock should not be there." Hmm, "should" is a loaded word. To say, "It's not what I expected" would perhaps be closer to the truth. But even this comment is beside the point because it does nothing toward solving the problem of how to move forward.

Second, it seems we start on a rock comparison exercise, which is equally beside the point. "It's a bigger rock than the last rock I remember." Maybe it is, maybe it isn't. So what? How does that have anything to do with moving forward? The answer, of course, is that it doesn't have anything to do with it. But that does not seem to stop us from thinking these unhelpful thoughts.

Third, we continue to compare and complain. "Other people don't have rocks in their paths." Maybe they do, maybe they don't. So what? "Let's compare my rock with theirs. Yes, mine is bigger." Maybe it is, maybe it isn't. Again, so what? "It's not fair." We are still missing the point, aren't we? However, I think by now we can all relate to what is going on here. With any luck, perhaps we are even smiling a bit. But what exactly is it that we are smiling about?

Hopefully, we are smiling at how we judge and fail to see the consequences of doing so. At best, judging wastes time, but at worst our judgments actually get in the way. Every moment spent doing a rock comparison exercise, or looking over our shoulder at our neighbors, contributes nothing to the business of moving forward. It is time wasted. Actually, it's worse than that because it distracts us and entrenches us in the current situation, thereby creating more of a problem than was ever there in the first place. What does water do? Of course, it just flows around the rock. And we could do exactly the same if we chose to. This is Option Two. "A rock? What rock? Oh, I see it's behind me."

The obstacle is not the rock; the obstacle lies within us. "If you close your mind in judgments and traffic with desires, your heart will be troubled. If you keep your mind from judging and aren't led by the senses, your heart will find peace" (chapter 52).

How often we do not keep our mind from judging. Every time we see something in terms of what we want it to be, rather than seeing it as it is, we are judging. The trouble is, we do not recognize that this is what we are doing. We think we are seeing reality as it is. But what we are usually doing is looking at reality in terms of what needs to be done to make it fulfill our desires or match up to our expectations. To see something as a "rock" is to label it. To see it as an "obstacle" is to judge it. We have now created a problem with which we can distract ourselves for as long as we like. This is what happens when we allow ourselves to "traffic with desires."

What if we simply accepted that some parts of any journey will be easy and other parts will be difficult? We could even go further and drop the labels "easy" and "difficult." Do they help us? Not really. What if we simply let go of the labels altogether? Water does not need to label anything as it flows on its journey to the sea. It just flows. If something is in the way, it just flows around it. It does not even matter what it was. Water does not call it anything. You can call it whatever you like. Just remember that while you are wondering what to call it, you are not flowing anywhere.

This chapter's observation reminds us to "be like water." If we did this, even if only a little more than we usually do, we would likely find our lives a lot less stressful. Things would certainly flow better. Maybe our hearts would even find peace.

24
THE WHOLE TRUTH

The truth is the whole.
It is beyond space, beyond time, beyond knowledge,
beyond distinctions between the known,
the unknown, and the unknowable.
It is all of them, all at once, all of the time.
Can we know the truth?

The pursuit of knowledge is an endless quest
to understand the whole in terms of parts.
We seek out new parts and define them
in terms of what we already know.
We make inroads into the unknown,
chart new territory, name the new parts,
and proudly bring them into the realm of the known.

Our knowledge expands, but it will always be limited
because it can never contain the unknown,
much less the unknowable or the limitless.
Thus the pursuit of knowledge is a noble pursuit,
but it is a pursuit nonetheless, and one without an end.

The whole truth is the known, the unknown, and the unknowable.
All we can do is be aware of it, accept it, embrace it.
It consists of no parts. It is everything all at once.
Including us.

To embrace the whole truth is to set aside the pursuit,
to come home and realize that we never left.

This observation asks if we can know the whole truth. The short answer is no. The longer answer depends on what we mean by "the whole truth." Let's explore.

The *Tao Te Ching* makes many references to knowledge. For example, "In the pursuit of knowledge, every day something is added" (chapter 48). However, accumulating knowledge may not lead where we think it does. While we may think it leads to understanding the truth, in fact it leads only to the accumulation of more knowledge—which is something much more limited. As a result, we hear words like "The more you know, the less you understand" (chapter 47) or "Those who know don't talk. Those who talk don't know" (chapter 56). Instead, we learn that understanding comes from doing the opposite of accumulating. "In the practice of the Tao, every day something is dropped" (chapter 48). Most likely this is not what we expected.

If knowledge is what we can wrap our heads around, then this observation starts by putting the whole truth somewhere on the other side of that. If we think we can understand space and time, then the whole truth is on the other side of that as well. None of this is to belittle knowledge; it can be very useful when applied. It is just that, in the grand scheme of things, knowledge is far more limited than we like to think.

At first glance, we might think there is what we know and what we do not yet know. As we pursue knowledge, we gradually convert the second into the first until the imaginary day when we will eventually know everything. This sounds simple, but this is the little scheme of things, as it were. This observation suggests there may be more to it than that. For a start, even on that imaginary day when we succeed in knowing it all, strictly speaking we would know only what there is to know. What if that turned out not to be everything? In this case, even if we knew everything, we still wouldn't know it all, would we?

"The pursuit of knowledge is an endless quest to understand the whole in terms of parts." The limit lies in the parts. "We make inroads into the unknown, chart new territory, name the new parts, and proudly bring them into the realm of the known. . . . The pursuit of knowledge is a noble pursuit." Yes, it is indeed a noble pursuit. But what if the sum of the parts is less than the whole truth? If it is, then our quest to "know it all" is doomed from the start. That is not say the quest is not worth undertaking. It is just to say it's worth getting a little more clarity on what we think we are doing and on what is possible as opposed to impossible.

If the whole truth is the Oneness/Wholeness that is everything, then it can never be understood in terms of parts. Oneness/Wholeness is simply Oneness/Wholeness. There is nothing more to say. However, this observation offers a shot at understanding this by saying a little more. "The whole truth is the known, the unknown, and the unknowable." At least this puts the pursuit of knowledge in a bigger context, because it includes what we can never know.

Is this a useful approach? I think it is, because it changes how we look at the parts. The *Tao Te Ching* tells us, "The Master views the parts with compassion, because he understands the whole" (chapter 39). To view the parts with compassion is to accept them exactly as they are. In other words, to see them as more than simply pieces of an incomplete puzzle, more than something to be fitted into the context of some bigger picture. To see them instead as something in and of themselves, already complete just the way they are. "The Master sees things as they are, without trying to control them. She lets them go their own way, and resides at the center of the circle" (chapter 29).

The pursuit of knowledge is what takes us away from the center of the circle. What if we are already at the center of the circle, even if we are unaware of it? What do we do then? "To embrace the whole truth is to set aside the pursuit, to come home and realize that we never left." The Master knows this. "Without opening your door, you can open your heart to the world. Without looking out your window, you can see the essence of the Tao" (chapter 47).

How often we think we know it all. If we pause for a moment, of course, we realize we do not in fact know it all. If we pause for two or three moments, perhaps we realize we can never know it all. The interesting question is this: What do we do now? Our usual response is to retreat back into the world that we can wrap our heads around, carry on with our familiar pursuit of knowledge, and enjoy the fruits of applying our ever-increasing knowledge.

Have you ever wondered about the unknowable? Or wondered about the Oneness/Wholeness that is everything? In other words, what we currently know, what we currently do not yet know, and what we can never know—all of them, all put together. What are we to do with that?

This chapter's observation suggests, "All we can do is be aware of it, accept it, embrace it. It consists of no parts. It is everything all at once. Including us." The *Tao Te Ching* says, "For lack of a better name, I call it the Tao" (chapter 25).

25
LET YOURSELF GO

The only thing between you and the moment is your self.
When you are in the moment, your self disappears.
It's as simple as that.

There are two ways this can happen.
The moment can be stronger than you are,
or you can let your self go.

When the moment is stronger than you are,
it likely catches you by surprise.
The beauty of a sunset is suddenly the only thing you're aware of.
The flow of a creative task carries you away.
You respond without thought to whatever's around you.

You can tell when this happens because we use words like
"I was lost in the moment" or "The moment took my breath away"
or "I needed to catch myself" or even "I needed to pinch myself."

We say things like this because
the moment was stronger than we were.
We forgot who we were. We forgot to breathe.
We pinched ourselves to remind us
that we were the one who could feel the pinching.
We could say our self was forced out of the moment.
It's as though it happened in spite of us.

The second way does not depend on the moment.
It depends on us—and it will happen because of us.
In this case, we are the ones who need to let our self go.
But this is not easy because our self will resist.

Most of the time our self is stronger than the moment.
It is in charge. It runs the show.
(We could even say it has a strong sense of self!)
So, how do we let go of our self?
Here's what makes this difficult.

If you try, it is your self that is doing the trying.
So, your self is still there. Trying will never work.
And trying hard will make it worse.
Letting your self go is never a matter of strength.
It is not a matter of willpower.
It is simply a choice in which the chooser disappears.

How do you make this choice?
Just open yourself to the moment
and then let it fill you up
until there is no room for your self.

Now you are in the moment.
Only this time, it didn't surprise you.
This time, you are not lost.
You are there on purpose.

Except there is no you.

Well-meaning people often give us advice like "Let yourself go" or "Things would go better if you got out of your own way" or "Don't be so full of yourself." This may cause us to think several things (maybe including "Did I ask for your advice?"). However, it may also cause us to think, "How do you know things would actually go better?" Or, "How full of myself do you think I am?" Or, "What if you're wrong?" Or, for that matter, "What if you're right?" Whatever else we may think, we can be sure our thoughts will always be noisy.

Nonetheless, we know that on some level there is truth in these comments. If we are honest with ourselves, we do sometimes get in our own way. I know I often overthink things or overanalyze them. Rather than trust what feels right, I tend to question what I feel to see if it withstands some test of rationality. And in doing this I am aware, on a nonrational level, that my questioning is sometimes exactly what gets in the way. The *Tao Te Ching* asks, "Do you have the patience to wait till your mud settles and the water is clear?" (chapter 15). My answer is often "No, I am too busy stirring up the mud."

However, at other times we know exactly what it feels like when the mud settles. These moments of clarity have one thing in common. We are fully present. No part of us is off somewhere else questioning the moment, wondering if another version of it would be better, figuring out what we might need to do to create that other version instead of this one. It all stops. There is just the moment. We are fully in it. It is all we are aware of. There is nothing else. The moment is everything there is. The water is crystal clear.

This observation suggests there are two ways this can happen. What they have in common is the result, which is that our noisy, questioning self is no longer there. How they differ is in the way in which this result happens. "The moment can be stronger than you are, or you can let your self go." This observation then looks at each of these ways in turn.

Examples of the moment being stronger than we are include being in awe of a sunset or being carried away in the flow of a creative task. Whatever is happening, we can tell it is not originating with us. It feels like something bigger than us. In the words of the observation, "We could say our self was forced out of the moment. It's as though it happened in spite of us."

The second way, however, depends on us. We are the ones who make it happen—or, to be more accurate, we are the ones who let it happen. However, to do this on purpose is not easy. In fact, it can be very difficult. And the reason it is difficult is that our self gets in the way. It actively resists, as it were. What is going on here?

The observation says, "Most of the time our self is stronger than the moment. It is in charge. It runs the show." When we try to let the self go, I think what is going on is that the self feels threatened and resists. It pushes back. The observation jokes, "We could even say it has a strong sense of self!" No kidding. You feel the pushback in the act of trying. The very fact that you have to try at all is evidence of the self in action. The self thinks it is fighting for its life. And, in a sense, it is. It is literally in self-preservation mode because, if it loses the fight, it will disappear.

Here's what the fight looks like. You think you need to set up the perfect conditions for letting your self go. So, you think you will just get a few more items crossed off your to-do list and then you will let yourself go. So you do your items and cross them off your list. You think you are ready now, so you give it a try. Oops, still not working. Never mind, let us try harder. However, it is still not working. Why not?

I think the clue lies in the casual phrase "never mind." It turns out this is exactly what we need to do. We need to put our mind aside. "The Master keeps her mind always at one with the Tao; that is what gives her her radiance" (chapter 21). The good news is, this is all we need to do. The bad news is that our mind prefers itself to the Tao. What can we do about that? The observation suggests the answer is not a matter of willpower, it is a matter of choice. "Letting yourself go . . . is simply a choice in which the chooser disappears." Easy to say. And exactly how do we do that? "Just open yourself to the moment, and then let it fill you up until there is no room for your self."

How often we occupy the moment. We are centered in ourselves, not centered in the Tao. We have a point of view, we see everything from it, and we are convinced that what we see is the way it is. When we are carried away in the flow of a creative task, we temporarily lose our point of view. We may even be unnerved by what feels like a lack of control. At the extreme, we may even think that looking at a sunset is a waste of time because we should be doing something more productive. For example, we should stop being "lost in the moment" and get back to work. Of course, these are exaggerated examples. But I think they make us aware of what is happening at the less extreme end of the scale—which is where we do most of our daily living.

We noted earlier that our self resists being let go because it feels it is fighting for its life. What if we reassured our self, like a little child, that it is simply not going to get our attention for a while? What if we told it there is nothing wrong with it, that it is not being abandoned? It is just that we need some time out, as it were. I almost said we need some time to ourselves—which is, of course, exactly what we do not need! Perhaps reassurance like this would take the struggle out of the moment.

This chapter's observation reminds us we can be fully present in the moment without being surprised or being lost in it. We can be there on purpose by choosing it. And when we are fully in the moment, we will recognize it because "you are there.... Except there is no you." At least, not for a while. The chooser has disappeared. What is left is the Tao.

26
WE ARE HERE TO AWAKEN

When we start our travel on the path,
we see ourselves as separate.
We believe we are here, our destination is there,
our journey will close the gap, and one day we will arrive.
We believe this is what our human lifetime is all about.
It feels very real to us.

But as we travel, we become aware
that this separateness is an illusion.
We discover there is no destination.
And the only journey is the journey
of becoming aware of this.

So, what is eternally real? We know it's not us
because sooner or later every human life comes to an end.
Instead, we discover that the only thing that is eternally real
is the Oneness/Wholeness that is everything.

It includes the here and there of the journey,
and us and everything that is now
or was or has yet to be in the future.
It is too big to grasp, too big even to name,
too big even to describe as "too big."
It's what Lao Tzu is talking about when he says,
"For lack of a better name, I call it the Tao."

To become aware of the Tao is like waking up.
As Thich Nhat Hanh says, "We are here
to awaken from the illusion of our separateness."
We are each a unique expression of the Tao,

alive for the length of a human life
in what we perceive as time.

That we are separate and time-bound is an illusion.
To awaken, and live boldly in awareness of this,
is what our human lifetime is all about.

The image of life as a journey is an old one. We have all likely heard the saying that life is about the journey itself, not about arriving at a destination. Yet we often live our lives as though we don't really believe that. Since real-world journeys start somewhere and end somewhere else, it is natural to see the purpose of a journey as being to get from one place to another. The journey is just a means to an end, which is to arrive somewhere else.

I think what happens when we apply the journey image to our lives is that we tend to keep too many of the details. Today we are no longer where we were yesterday. Tomorrow we will be somewhere new. So it appears we really are going somewhere. Of course, we know we are not actually travelling from one geographical place to another (most of the time). Instead, we often see ourselves as in a process of becoming. Nonetheless, I think trouble starts because we become distracted by some place we have not yet arrived at, or by something we have not yet become. Once distracted, we lose sight of where we are right now. This observation explores what happens when we do that.

Journeys, by definition, separate the start from the finish. We are going somewhere where we are not—at least, not yet. Separation is the gap. In the words of the observation, "We believe we are here, our destination is there, our journey will close the gap, and one day we will arrive." It all feels very real to us. But how real is it? Is it just a temporary illusion? In other words, is it merely real enough for the time being, or is it eternally real? We don't know. Let's see if we can figure it out.

We know we are temporary because one day we will die, and nobody knows for sure what lies beyond. So, whatever is eternally real is going to have to include whatever is on the other side of the temporary. We can wonder what else needs to be included. But the end of all our wondering is to "discover that the only thing that is eternally real is the Oneness/Wholeness that is everything." Anything less will be part of the illusion. The Master understands this. "He dwells in reality, and lets all illusions go" (chapter 38).

What is there to say about the eternally real? The answer is, not much. For a start, when we try to talk about it, we discover that words do not work very well. The eternally real "includes the here and there of the journey, and us and everything that is now or was or has yet to be in the future." What is a good word for that? Lao Tzu gives up. "For lack of a better name, I call it the Tao" (chapter 25).

So, what are we doing here? What is our place in the eternally real? "Every being in the universe is an expression of the Tao" (chapter 51). So, according to the *Tao Te Ching*, that is what we are doing here. "We are each a unique expression of the Tao, alive for the length of a human life in what we perceive as time." Are we separate? No. Are we going anywhere? No. What can we hold on to? Nothing, not even the journey. "The Master gives himself up to whatever the moment brings. He knows that he is going to die, and he has nothing left to hold on to: no illusions in his mind, no resistances in his body" (chapter 50).

So how does the Master live in the meantime? "He doesn't think about his actions; they flow from the core of his being. He holds nothing back from life; therefore he is ready for death" (chapter 50). The Master is aware he is going nowhere. He is aware that separateness is an illusion. He does not journey in order to get to the other side of the illusion. After all, if it is an illusion, there is no other side. He is already there. There is nowhere to go. So, what does he do? He simply lets go of the illusion and dwells in reality instead. As Thich Nhat Hanh says, "We are here to awaken from the illusion of our separateness."

How often we dwell inside the illusion. The here and now feels very real to us. And for all practical, temporary, time-bound purposes it is. Our experience of reality is as real as it gets. The trouble starts when we try to hold on to it or shape reality into something we think will better satisfy our desires. To do that is to live inside the illusion. It is to be asleep without knowing it. It is to dream and believe that the dream is real.

After all, only in the dream can we hold on to things. How do we know? Because when we try to do that in reality, we discover we cannot succeed. If we appear to succeed, then we soon discover we can do so only for a little while. The Master holds on to nothing, "thus has nothing to lose. What he desires is non-desire; what he learns is to unlearn" (chapter 64). If we believe we can hold on, then we are dreaming. Trying to hold on is something we have not "unlearned" yet.

What would happen if we lived with only the eternally real in mind? What if we let go of everything that appears to be fleeting and temporary? For example, possessions, money, security, the opinions of others—anything that is here one day and gone the next. In fact, we might as well include our self in that, because we too are here one day and gone the next. What if we let go of our self? What if we used our lives simply to explore what it is to be a "unique expression of the Tao" for as long as our human life happens to be?

This chapter's observation reminds us that "to awaken, and live boldly in awareness of this, is what our human lifetime is all about."

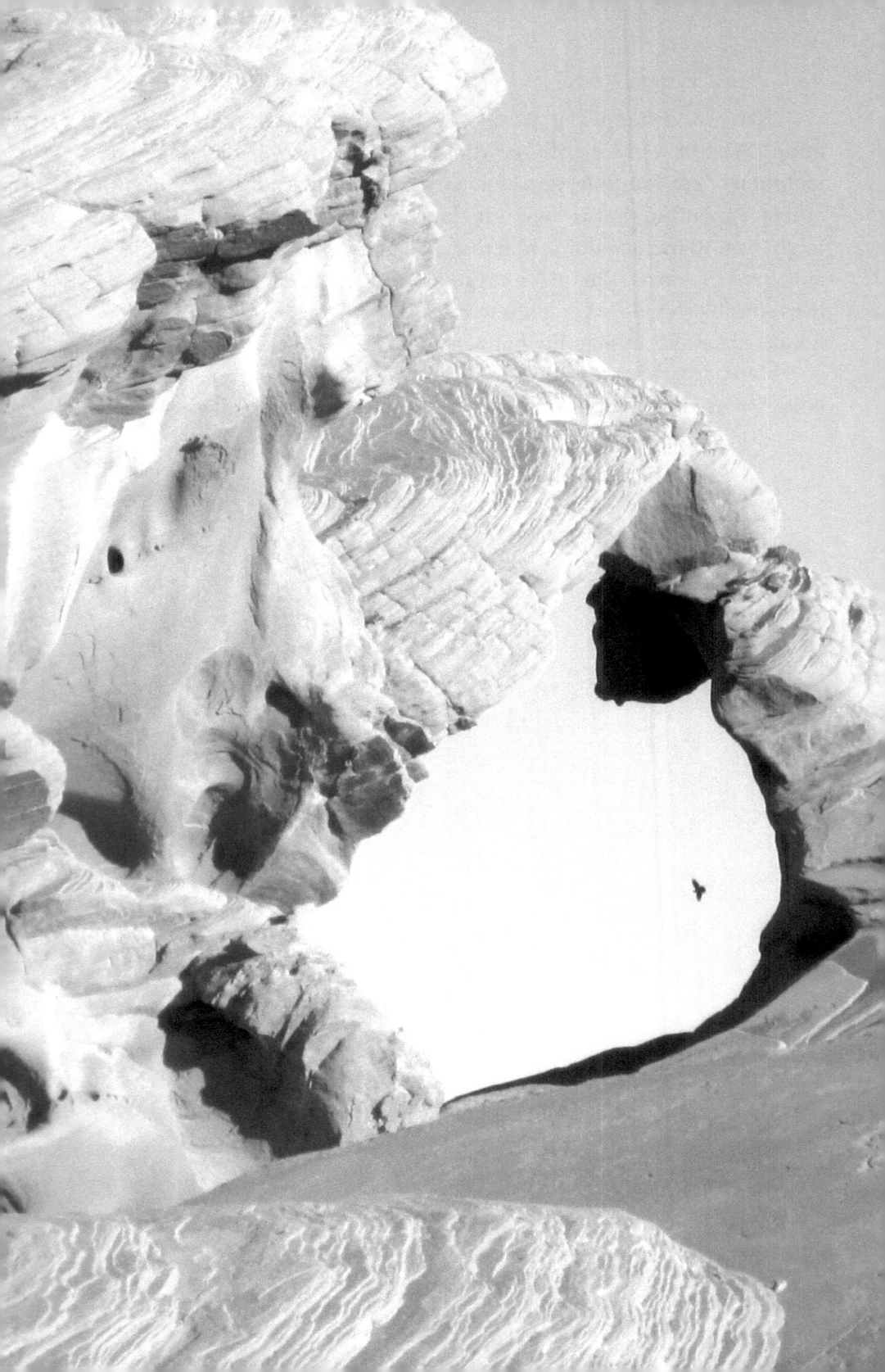

27
INSIDE THE DREAM

Life is a dream in which we think we are awake.
But to think anything at all is to be asleep.
To be awake is to be aware of the dream even as we live it.

Inside the dream, our mind is full of thoughts.
Thought is king. It rules the day because
we let our thoughts about things direct our actions.
Judgments. Opinions. Desires. Expectations.
So many thoughts. Pulling us this way and that.
Acting as if our thoughts are real is what keeps us asleep.

To wake up, all we need do is put thought aside.
When we empty our mind of all thoughts,
thought can no longer be king–and we will no longer be asleep.

Suddenly we see things as they really are, not as we think they are.
No judging. No opinions. No desires. No expectations.
No being pulled this way and that. Just stillness and quiet.
What do we see?

We see reality at one with itself.
Everything at one with itself. Including us.
Except there is no thing, no self, no us.
Just Oneness/Wholeness. Hidden in plain sight.
All the time. Eternally present. Eternally real.

That's it. Now you have seen what is there all the time.
Soon you will go back and live inside the dream again.
What you have seen will disappear.
Once more, it will be hidden in plain sight.

Just remember, at any time, you can see it again.
All you need do is empty your mind.
When thoughts no longer pull you this way and that
you will naturally re-center yourself in the stillness and quiet.
This is how to live inside the dream
and be wide awake.

The idea that life is a dream is an old and familiar one. Are we asleep or are we awake? Equally old is the philosophical observation that the answer is not obvious. However, the observation in this chapter explores a different aspect. It looks at three questions. First, if we are asleep, then what is it that keeps us asleep and dreaming? Second, what can we do to wake up? Third, what do we see when we are awake?

The observation starts by noting that our mind is typically full of thoughts. "Judgments. Opinions. Desires. Expectations. So many thoughts. Pulling us this way and that." Being aware of our thoughts and acting on them certainly makes us feel we are awake. After all, if we are to satisfy our desires and fulfill expectations, then we need to do something deliberate about it—and we cannot do that when we are asleep. Therefore, as we spend a lot of our time acting deliberately, we must surely be awake. However, this observation suggests that "acting as if our thoughts are real is what keeps us asleep." That does not seem to make sense. So let's explore.

The *Tao Te Ching* contains many words of caution about thoughts. "Thoughts weaken the mind. Desires wither the heart" (chapter 12). "Stop thinking and end your problems" (chapter 20). The trouble with thoughts is that we tend not to question them. This is why they can so easily weaken our minds and cause problems. However, this observation suggests thought does more than that. It suggests that acting on unquestioned thoughts is like taking orders from a king. Thought "rules the day" and we blindly follow its orders, as it were.

You would think we could tell whether or not we're doing this. But it seems often we cannot. And, if you think about it, blindly following anything involves having our eyes closed—which is also what being asleep looks like. The first question was, What keeps us asleep and dreaming? This observation suggests that the answer is allowing ourselves to be ruled by thought.

The second question was, What can we do to wake up? The short answer is to stop being ruled, to stop blindly following orders, to stop treating thought as king. The longer answer involves recognizing that there is a time and place for thought; it is just not everywhere and not all of the time. There is a time for putting thought aside. And the moment we do that is the moment we wake up. How do we know we are awake? "No judging. No opinions. No desires. No expectations. No being pulled this way and that. Just stillness and quiet." This is the peace the *Tao Te Ching* talks about. "Empty your mind of all thoughts. Let your heart be at peace" (chapter 16).

The third question was, What do we see when we are awake? "We see things as they really are, not as we think they are. . . . We see reality at one with itself. Everything at one with itself. Including us. Except there is no thing, no self, no us. Just Oneness/Wholeness." What is going on here? What is Oneness/Wholeness, and why don't we see it all the time?

The reason we do not see Oneness/Wholeness all the time is simple. Thought gets in the way. Thought separates, divides, splits Oneness into a thousand parts, which then all have to be named so we can talk about them, desire them, chase after them, and worry about them. What if all this activity is an illusion, a distraction? What if it none of it is real at all? What if it is part of the dream? Could being ruled by our thoughts be the very thing that keeps us asleep? (By the way, isn't it interesting how many thoughts occur to us when we question thought itself? And of course, each question is a thought. Thought just doesn't want to let go of us, does it?)

A final question might be, Is all this thinking the reason why we cannot see the Oneness/Wholeness of all things, which is there all the time? This observation suggests the answer is yes. Oneness/Wholeness is always there, whether we can see it or not—it is simply "hidden in plain sight." What's more, we are the ones keeping it hidden as long as our eyes are closed. Now you see it. Now you don't. It depends on whether you are awake or asleep.

What this observation suggests is that whether you are awake or asleep is up to you. To see it, all you need do is wake up. To wake up, all you need do is empty your mind of all thoughts and trust what you become aware of. Alternatively, you can stay asleep and let yourself be ruled by your thoughts. You choose. But choose with your whole heart, because if you pause to think about it, you risk falling asleep again.

How often we stay asleep. How often we are not even aware we have a choice. How often we live our days being pulled this way and that, blindly following orders from our thoughts. We desire this, we chase after that, we regret things we can do nothing about, we worry about a future we cannot control. We can live weeks, months, and years like this.

Have you ever noticed what happens when you experience stillness, quiet, and peace? Most likely one thing you are not doing is thinking about it. Peace is simply present, and you are a part of it, nothing is missing. "When you realize there is nothing lacking, the whole world belongs to you" (chapter 44). Emptying your mind of thoughts is not about forcing them out; it is about simply letting them go. When you do that, you reveal the stillness, quiet, and peace that has been there all along, "hidden in plain sight." Oneness/Wholeness is always there. It is there even when we are asleep and dreaming. It's just that we cannot see it with our eyes closed.

This chapter's observation reminds us, "This is how to live inside the dream and be wide awake."

28
FOCUS ON THE STEPS

Making progress is not a spectator sport.
If it were, we could sit back and watch.
Progress would happen all on its own.
Trouble is, it doesn't work that way.
Instead, our active participation is required.

The journey of a thousand miles starts with a single step.
And we're the ones who have to take that step.
What's more, we need to follow it with many more
to cover even the first mile.

As we journey, we discover some steps turn out
to move us forward more quickly than others.
But we cannot always tell which steps these will be.
The only way to find out is to take them and see.
Our part is simply to show up ready to take steps every day.

So, don't think about whether a given step is big or small,
or difficult or easy, or will or will not produce
exactly the result you want as quickly as you want.
Thinking never moves you forward.
Only taking steps moves you forward.
And, most of the time, the next step is obvious.

Sometimes we think we need a perfect plan.
But plans contain assumptions.
And perfect plans contain too many.
Take a step and the world will tell you
which assumptions were true and which were not.
Experience is better than assumptions.

So, focus on the next step, the whole step,
and nothing but the step. Then take it.
Then take the next one. And the next. Persist.
Show up. Do the work.
It's not complicated.

This observation is about moving forward, and that always involves taking action. The *Tao Te Ching* contains the well-known saying "The journey of a thousand miles starts from beneath your feet" (chapter 64). I think the point is not so much that the journey is a thousand miles long but that it starts from beneath your feet, not someone else's feet. You are the one who has to actually put one foot in front of the other. However, taking steps is not always easy. This observation explores why.

The observation starts by noting that it is always easier to watch others taking action. A good example is watching sports, something many of us like to do. Sometimes we can do what the players do, but the players do it much better. Other times we watch in awe as others do things we know we could never do. But in both cases, we are spectators, not players. And spectators are never where the action is.

Taking action is always an act of discovery because we do not know exactly what will happen. We might wonder why that should matter. Why don't we just take the step and find out? I think the answer is that, on some level, we want assurance in advance. Ideally, we want our progress to be easy and effortless, yet experience tells us this may or may not turn out to be the case. Of course, that need not hold us back but often it does. Why should this be so?

Wanting to know in advance suggests our mind is not open. For some reason, it seems we find openness uncomfortable. Instead, we typically replace openness with some sort of expectation. Expectation is usually based on our past experience, which, as we have seen, is not always good. So, we hesitate because, on some level, perhaps we fear a repeat of something that was not easy and effortless last time. We wonder what exactly will happen when things take their course this time. The truth is that we don't know. And what holds us back is fear that we cannot control the outcome.

Here is where we can learn from the Master. "Therefore the Master takes action by letting things take their course. He remains as calm at the end as at the beginning" (chapter 64). "Acting with no expectations, leading and not trying to control: this is the supreme virtue" (chapter 10). Note there is no reference to fear; and the only mention of expectations is that we do not need them. In the words of this observation, "Our part is simply to show up ready to take steps every day." Whatever we may think, it turns out that being able to control the outcome is not required. Having an open mind is the only thing that matters.

None of this is to say we cannot learn from experience. After all, it is experience that tells us some of the steps on our journey will be easy while others will be difficult. Sometimes we can tell in advance; sometimes we cannot. Often, we can deliberately stack the odds in favor of the outcome we want. We call this planning and there is nothing wrong with it. But, as this observation notes, "Thinking never moves you forward. Only taking steps moves you forward." Sooner or later we have to take a step, and when we do, it is best to be like the Master and "let things take their course."

There is a saying that planning is bringing the future into the present so we can do something about it now. I think this is a useful saying because there is usually a certain amount of planning we can do. Sometimes even only a little thought can show that some courses of action have little chance of success. The question is, How much thought do we need? How much planning should we do? This observation suggests we sometimes err on the side of too much because we are in pursuit of the "perfect plan." What is going on here?

All plans deal with the future, so they contain assumptions for the good reason that the future has not happened yet. And there is nothing wrong with this. The question is when to stop making assumptions and when to start acting. In other words, when to stop wondering what we might do if a particular step turns out to be difficult or easy, and when to start finding out. "Sometimes we think we need a perfect plan. But plans contain assumptions. And perfect plans contain too many." What is going on here is that we are focusing on the plan instead of on taking the step.

How often we want assurance that everything will go smoothly. Sometimes it is as if we want to know all the possible outcomes so we can build every appropriate detail into the plan no matter what happens. If the stakes are high, we may feel justified in our approach. But, most of the time, is this really the case? Sometimes a step is exactly what it looks like, just a step. As this observation says, "Take a step and the world will tell you which assumptions were true and which were not."

Have you ever wondered when to stop planning? After all, the purpose of the journey is not to collect lists of assumptions and then examine them in hindsight to see which turned out to be true and which false. The purpose of the journey is far simpler than that and far more important—it is to move forward. Learning from experience and planning have their place, but nothing happens until we do the work of taking the next step. "So, focus on the next step, the whole step, and nothing but the step. Then take it."

This chapter's observation reminds us that what matters most is to "show up. Do the work. It's not complicated." Sometimes there is less to taking a step than meets the eye. It all depends what we focus on. Hence, "focus on the steps." After all, we may have a thousand miles to go!

29
JUST FOR TODAY

Here I am, ready to let the universe unfold through me.

Just for today, may I see my path—and believe enough to accept it.
Just for today, may I listen—and be trusting enough of what I hear.
Just for today, may I know what to do—and be willing enough to act.
Just for today, may I believe, trust, and act.

I know there is much I am capable of.
I know there is a difference I can make in this world.
It is as if the universe has dreams for me
and is constantly giving me all I need to make those
      dreams come true.

But I also know I cannot see all there is to be seen.
I do not know all there is to be known.
I do not understand all there is to be understood.
It is as if I need the universe to help me do my part—
      which is simply
to believe, to trust, and to act, one day at a time.

I accept what I am ready for today.
I trust in what I will be ready for tomorrow.
I allow wisdom to grow within me.
I embrace today's steps on my life's journey.
I let those dreams for me come true.

Here I am, ready to let the universe unfold through me.

This observation seems a little unusual. It sounds like a prayer. The *Tao Te Ching* contains many observations but none of them are prayers. What is this about? I think it is about what happens when we let go of thinking that we can see, know, and understand everything. When this happens, we become open to everything all around us, including the part we can play in how it unfolds. This observation simply expresses the wish that this be so.

However, it is not a vague wish. If anything, it seems to be directed toward someone or something. It also seems to acknowledge that to make the wish come true will involve some sort of active collaboration on the part of the wisher. If this adds up to a prayer, then this observation is a prayer. However, the label matters less than what the wish is about.

The wisher clearly thinks their part is not an easy one. Four lines start with the words "Just for today." So it seems the wisher hopes to succeed in doing their part at least for one day. Tomorrow they can always hope again. After all, lives are lived one day at a time. So, just for today, what do they think their part is? What follows is a list of three responses to life that they hope to make: belief, trust, and having the willingness to act. Let's look at each in turn.

If life is a journey and we are on a path, then one of the things that makes the journey difficult is when it is hard to see the path. The *Tao Te Ching* acknowledges this difficulty when it says, "The path into the light seems dark, the path forward seems to go back, the direct path seems long" (chapter 41). What do we do when confronted with such an elusive path? This observation suggests that when we cannot see it, we need simply to believe in it.

The *Tao Te Ching* goes further and suggests that if we are looking for the path we will never find it. "When you look for it, there is nothing to see. When you listen for it, there is nothing to hear" (chapter 35). This brings us to the second response to life, which is simply to trust. If we are prepared to believe and trust what we cannot be sure of seeing or hearing, then what is our part when it comes to taking action? This is the third response, and the observation suggests all we need do is "be willing enough to act."

It is important to note we do not start with nothing. Depending on how long we have been alive and how well know ourselves, we all know we are capable of at least some things. We all know there is at least some difference we can make in this world before we die. But where did our capabilities come from? We may have discovered and developed our talents, but it does not take much humility to be aware that we did not create them. Nor do we entirely create the situations in which we can express them.

However, regardless of where our talents and the opportunities for expressing them come from, they represent nothing but potential until we recognize them for what they are. In the words of the observation, "It is as if the universe has dreams for me and is constantly giving me all I need to make those dreams come true." If we have already been given all we need, then what holds us back from making those dreams come true? (By the way, the key words in the quote are "as if"—there's no suggestion that the universe is really dreaming about anything, much less dreaming about us!)

I think what holds us back is wanting to see, know, and understand. It seems we always want to see more, to know more, to understand more. But would this really make a difference? Would we ever see, know, and understand enough? I think the answer is no. We are missing the point. The point is that right now, "I have everything I need to do my part—which is simply to believe, to trust, and to act, one day at a time."

The observation closes by spelling this out in more detail. Our part is to accept, trust, allow, embrace, and let. The *Tao Te Ching* sums this up by saying, "Open yourself to the Tao, then trust your natural responses; and everything will fall into place" (chapter 23). In other words, our part is not to see clearly and know with certainty what to do. It is to become aware that we are part of something much greater than we are—the Tao. This observation refers to the Tao as the "universe." Hence the words "Here I am, ready to let the universe unfold through me."

How often we feel we cannot see the path clearly, we cannot hear clearly, and we do not know enough. How seldom we feel comfortable with words like "accept," "trust," "allow," "embrace," and "let." I think we want to know more so that when we act, we can trust ourselves to be able to command and control the outcome. In contrast, "The Master observes the world but trusts his inner vision. He allows things to come and go. His heart is open as the sky" (chapter 12). This is what letting go looks like, and it is the opposite of command and control.

What if we do not need to gather information from the outside so that we can trust ourselves? What if it is not ourselves that we need to trust? What if everything is already taken care of, as it were? "The Tao gives birth to all beings, nourishes them, maintains them, cares for them, comforts them, protects them, takes them back to itself" (chapter 51). What if instead of trusting ourselves we trusted the Tao?

This chapter's observation reminds us that there may be less to trusting the Tao than we think. We may not even need to gather information about it. Perhaps all we need to do is "simply to believe, to trust, and to act, one day at a time."

30
NOW IS ALL THERE IS

Now is all there is.

The moment ago, was.
The moment to come, will be.
The only moment that is, is the one that is here right now.

You can look back at the past and learn from it.
You can look forward to the future and plan to influence it.
Time spent doing this need not be wasted.
But the past and the future are not the place to dwell.

The place to dwell is in the present moment.
You are using it right now as you read these words.
You are always using the present moment. It is always here.
The question is, Where are you?

So, look back and learn. Look forward and plan.
But then stop—sooner than you think.
Do not dwell in the places you cannot be.
Let it all go. And show up here, now.
Be present in this moment.

Now is all there is.

It is an old saying that anything other than this present moment is an illusion. Yet it is surprising how much of the time we live as though we don't really believe that. Instead, our everyday world gives us lots of reasons to see the present moment in what we like to think of as the broader context of time. While context certainly has its uses, it is not always helpful. This observation explores the extent to which any context, regardless of its broadness, is also part of the illusion.

The observation starts by looking back at what we call the past and then looking forward to what we call the future. The past is "the moment ago" and the future is "the moment to come." In an everyday sense, there is nothing unusual or difficult about either of these concepts. Every day we get reminders that by tomorrow, today will have become yesterday. But the trouble is that both yesterday and tomorrow are exactly that, concepts. They are never times in which we can actually be present. "The only moment that is, is the one that is here right now." So, why do we spend any time going back and forth to times where we cannot be present?

The *Tao Te Ching* tells us, "The Master gives himself up to whatever the moment brings. He knows that he is going to die, and he has nothing left to hold on to: no illusions in his mind" (chapter 50). Whenever we visit the past or the future, the one thing we are not doing is giving ourselves up to "whatever the moment brings." Instead, we are busy somewhere else.

The observation acknowledges that "time spent doing this need not be wasted." After all, we can learn from the past—and to do that we have to spend some time there. We can also build on what we learn by making plans for the future—and to do that we have to spend some time there too. But in both cases, the question is, How much time? We might wonder why this matters. The reason is that "the past and the future are not the place to dwell." If dwelling is where we spend most of our time, then it matters where we choose to do it.

The trouble is that, unless we are aware of it, we typically dwell wherever our mind likes to go. If that is anywhere other than the present moment, the *Tao Te Ching* suggests that we are entering the illusion. If we do so, then wherever we are, it is not where reality is.

Thus the Master "dwells in reality, and lets all illusions go" (chapter 38). The Master is always right here, right now. And, for that matter, this observation points out that so are you. You are right here in this present moment. "You are using it right now as you read these words." This is not a trick. It is simply a statement of something that is real right now. In this particular moment, there is nothing else.

We have seen that it can be useful to visit the past to learn, and to visit the future to plan. After all, we discover early in life that our actions can influence what we experience. We also discover that what we experience is seldom entirely up to us, and so we learn the difference between influence and control. While we may prefer control, we learn to recognize when we can do no more than influence. And sometimes we cannot even influence very much. But how much of our time do we spend doing this rather than simply being in the present moment? In other words, recognizing we can do no more than influence, where do we choose to dwell?

To dwell in either the past or the future is to risk becoming drawn not only into the illusion but also into what the *Tao Te Ching* calls the "turmoil of beings." Looking backwards to the past to learn, we risk dwelling there and regretting. Looking forward to the future to plan, we risk dwelling there and worrying about what might happen. Regret and worry are part of the turmoil. In both cases, our mind is full of thoughts and our heart is not at peace.

Regardless of where we are, the *Tao Te Ching* tells us how to return to the present moment. "Empty your mind of all thoughts. Let your heart be at peace. Watch the turmoil of beings, but contemplate their return. Each separate being in the universe returns to the common source. Returning to the source is serenity. If you don't realize the source, you stumble in confusion and sorrow" (chapter 16). The source is timeless, and the only timeless moment we can ever experience is the present one. In the present moment there is no stumbling, no confusion, no sorrow. And the present moment is always here, which means the source is always here. In the words of this observation, "The question is, Where are you?"

How often we are anywhere but in the present moment. It is surprising how much of the time we wonder, What if something had happened differently in the past, or, What if something in particular were to happen in the future? If you want to keep your mind busy, try asking any question that starts with "What if?" For me, at least, it works every time. Let's try it now.

What if we emptied our mind of all thoughts? What if we stepped out of the turmoil of beings? The answer is, we would discover that our heart would be at peace. Here and now is where the source is. And whether we are busy in the past or the future, we can return to the source any time we choose. "Returning to the source is serenity" (chapter 16). This is the place to dwell.

This chapter's observation reminds us that to dwell anywhere else is to live in the illusion. "Let it all go. And show up here, now. Be present in this moment. Now is all there is." This is to live in the timeless reality of now.

31
IN THE MOMENT

There are two places to dwell.
In the moment, and outside the moment.
Which do you choose?
Dwell outside the moment and your self runs the show.
Dwell in the moment and you disappear.

Outside the moment, there is separation
between you and the moment.
There is a gap in which your self exists.
Here dwell thought and all that thought creates.
Expectation and judgment, worry and regret, fear and sorrow.
At other times joyful anticipation and hope.
But always, so much distraction. So much noise.

In the moment, there is no separation.
No gap. No room for self or thought.

You are not silent; there is only silence.
You are not aware; there is only awareness.
You are not separate; there is only oneness.

In the moment, you disappear.
There is only the moment.
It was there all along.

There are only two places to dwell.
Which do you choose?

This observation builds on the last one, "Now Is All There Is." The last observation explored how we enter an illusion whenever we live anywhere but in the present moment. We saw that brief trips into the past could be useful for learning, and that brief trips into the future could be useful for planning. But the point was that neither the past nor the future was "the place to dwell." This observation explores how the illusion works and what we need to do avoid dwelling there.

As in the previous observation, this one notes you are either in the present moment or not. It doesn't matter whether you are on a trip into the past or into the future, either way you are not in the present. What this observation does is focus on "you." It asks: Who is it that is doing the traveling? Who is it that is either in the present moment or not? This observation suggests that when you are in the present moment, "you" are in fact nowhere. "Dwell outside the moment and your self runs the show. Dwell in the moment and you disappear." What is going on here?

A clue lies in the following quote from the *Tao Te Ching*: "The Master gives himself up to whatever the moment brings" (chapter 50). If we ask, What exactly has the Master given up? the answer is "himself." What happens when you give yourself up is that your "self" disappears. Before you gave yourself up, where were you? The short answer is that you were not in the present moment. The longer answer is that you existed in what this observation calls a "gap." And, what's more, the gap is the only place you can exist. Your self cannot exist anywhere else. Let's explore this gap.

"Outside the moment, there is separation between you and the moment. There is a gap in which your self exists." Inside and outside cannot exist without separation. In fact, nothing can exist without separation—perhaps we should say that "no thing" can exist without separation. This is because separate things are the terms in which we see the world. This is the world of knowledge, and it has many useful applications of which we are typically quite proud. "In the pursuit of knowledge, every day something is added" (chapter 48). The trouble is that thought creates other things as well as knowledge.

While you exist in the gap, so do "thought and all that thought creates. Expectation and judgment, worry and regret, fear and sorrow. At other times joyful anticipation and hope." These can be much less useful than knowledge. "Always, so much distraction. So much noise." We become easily sidetracked by what we do, what we say, and what we try to control or hold on to or remember.

Compare this with what the Master does. "The Master acts without doing anything and teaches without saying anything. Things arise and she lets them come; things disappear and she lets them go. She has but doesn't possess, acts but doesn't expect. When her work is done, she forgets it. That is why it lasts forever" (chapter 2). What the Master does is show us what it is like not to live in the gap but, instead, to live in the moment. The Master is not sidetracked by anything.

This observation notes, "In the moment, there is no separation. No gap. No room for self or thought." This is not the space in which we will make discoveries about our material world, or invent new ways to control disease, or design a city or a cathedral, or create great works of art or literature. This space can certainly be wonderful in its own way, but all of it involves standing back and thinking. And the moment we stand back and think is the moment we create the gap in which the self exists that is doing the thinking.

What is in the moment if we do not stand back? This observation describes what is there when you are not. For example, it is not you that is silent—it cannot be, because you are not there. What is there is only silence. It is not you that is aware—because you are not there. What is there is only awareness. It is not you that is not separate—because you are not there. What is there is only oneness. Silence. Awareness. Oneness. Nothing else—no thing else, if you like. "There is only the moment. It was there all along." And in the moment lies serenity. As the *Tao Te Ching* observes, "Do your work, then step back. The only path to serenity" (chapter 9).

How often we do not step back. As a result, how often we live in a world of "expectation and judgment, worry and regret, fear and sorrow." The reason we do not step back is quite simple; it is because our self is running the show. Our self typically takes itself very seriously. Our self has a vested interest in the actions it directs. Much of what we do is an attempt to satisfy desires or fulfill expectations. Our self wants to stick around to make sure it enjoys the results. Whenever we do something as a means to an end, we do not step back, because the end is exactly what we are interested in. And so we live outside the moment. We live in the gap, anticipating the future or, more often than not, worrying about it.

Have you ever noticed yourself disappear in the moment? Once again, I will use the familiar example of being present at an awesome sunset. You did not create the sunset to satisfy some desire of yours. Nor do you control, or even influence, the sunset. The sunset is what it is whether or not you are there. When you witness the sunset, you are simply in its presence. And when you are fully in its presence, you discover that "you" are not there. There is only the sunset. There is no separation between you and the sunset. There is no separation. Only oneness. The gap has disappeared, and "you" have disappeared along with it.

We all know we cannot spend our lives watching sunsets. However, we can spend much more of our lives not separating ourselves from this experience of oneness. When we do, we find that all manner of conflict and difficulty disappear. Instead of living inside our own heads, we live in harmony with the Tao.

This chapter's observation reminds us, "There are only two places to dwell. Which do you choose?" Perhaps the answer is simply to acknowledge that we live in both places from time to time, but also to be aware that we have a choice. When we experience distraction, we can always choose to let go of ourselves, disappear into the moment for a while, and experience serenity. And we don't even need to wait for a sunset.

32
WHAT IF

We don't know where we came from,
and we don't know where we're going.
It feels as though we're on a journey
passing through a world of things.

Time appears real.
But today exists only in the context of yesterday and tomorrow.
The world of things appears real.
But things exist only because we distinguish them
      from one another.
We exist only because we distinguish ourselves from everything else.

But what if context and distinctions exist only because
we see ourselves as separate from what we observe?
What if the observer and the observed are one and the same?
What if there is no separation from Oneness?
What if there is only Oneness?

The only thing we know for sure
is that we are right here right now.

What if this moment is the only reality?
What if everything else is an illusion?
Separation, context, distinctions—all illusions.

What if we simply lived in awareness of this?
What if we simply lived in the Oneness?
What if we simply lived?

What if . . .

This observation takes another look at the metaphor of life as a journey. It explores the experience of our human lives and wonders how much of the journey is real. What if less of it is real than we think? In fact, what if none of it is real? But we are getting ahead of ourselves already.

Journeys are a useful metaphor because the experience of a journey is a familiar one. We start somewhere, we travel over time, and we end up somewhere else. Being in one place, feeling time pass and then being in another place, is a very real experience. Similarly, time always travels forward; it is not an option to go backwards; nor is it useful to act as though time does not exist. Another reason our journey feels real is because we see different things around us, and they come and go. What is around us today, including people, is not the same as what was around us yesterday. Things change. In fact, we live our entire lives navigating through this "world of things" in the course of what we experience as time.

How then do we make sense of what the Master does? The *Tao Te Ching* tells us that "the Master travels all day without leaving home" (chapter 26). What does he think he is doing? How can he get anywhere? Yet, apparently, he does. "The Master arrives without leaving, sees the light without looking, achieves without doing a thing" (chapter 47). How can he arrive in the same instant that he leaves? What happened to time? What is going on here? Let's take another look at our journey.

This observation suggests, "Time appears real. But today exists only in the context of yesterday and tomorrow." So, it helps to ask the question, Who introduced the so-called context? The answer is, we did. "The world of things appears real. But things exist only because we distinguish them from one another." Who introduced the distinctions? We did. Each time, we are the ones separating things, distinguishing them, and naming them. We even do it to ourselves. "We exist only because we distinguish ourselves from everything else."

So now the observation asks the big What if? question: "What if context and distinctions exist only because we see ourselves as separate from what we observe?" The question seems strange because the answer seems obvious. Of course we see ourselves as separate because we *are* separate. We are inside and the world is outside. Things really *are* different from one another, which is why we give them different names. It doesn't start with us. It starts with the way the world is. Or so we think.

But this observation asks, What if it's the other way around? What if things are different only *because* we give them different names? What if none of the distinctions are real? What if it's all our doing? The simplest answer is to say that if that is true, then it doesn't make any sense. And on a practical, everyday level, that is completely correct. It does not make sense. Things are real. Time does pass. We are born. We die. What's not real about that?

But perhaps the Master is aware of something we don't know. What if there is something going on that is bigger than our practical, everyday level? The *Tao Te Ching* makes a distinction between the world we live in and what is "eternally real." It acknowledges what we observe and experience, but simply suggests it is not eternally real—instead it is a world of what it calls "manifestations." How so?

"The tao that can be told is not the eternal Tao. The name that can be named is not the eternal Name. The unnamable is the eternally real. Naming is the origin of all particular things. Free from desire, you realize the mystery. Caught in desire, you see only the manifestations" (chapter 1). This suggests not only do we live in a world of manifestations, but also we are the ones who create them. It is the manifestations that are temporary; they are what come and go. The only thing that is eternally real is Oneness/Wholeness.

So, what happens when we stop naming things and making distinctions between them? The answer is that the manifestations disappear and only the Tao remains. The Master is aware of this—and that is exactly what she does. She simply lets it all go. "She is detached from all things; that is why she is one with them. Because she has let go of herself, she is perfectly fulfilled" (chapter 7). Why is she one with all things? The answer is, because only the Tao remains. This is how she arrives without leaving. This is how she travels all day without leaving home. This is how she dwells in the Tao.

How often we live as though what we experience is real. What makes letting it go so difficult is that it feels so real. Separation, context, distinctions, they all feel real—and so does the passage of time. It feels as though this is what our human lifetime is all about. Equally true, however, is that we very often do not feel "perfectly fulfilled." This is why we can learn from the Master.

Have you ever simply let yourself go? When you do, you make an interesting discovery. Thoughts about how anything should be any different from exactly the way it is simply stop. You accept that everything simply is what it is. After all, why would you compare anything with an imaginary version of what it should be? The very notion of "should be" is what is not real. The eternally real is what is here right now. The Tao is always here. And we dwell in it the moment we let everything else go.

This chapter's observation reminds us that the more we think about it, the more we enter the world of manifestations. What if it is all much simpler than we think? What if we let go of the distinctions and "simply lived in the Oneness?" What if awareness of this Oneness, and dwelling in it, are in fact what our human lifetime is all about? The answer is ... No, don't even think about it.

33
THIS WORLD

For the time being, we live in a world of things
and we experience the passage of time.

We see things as being out there,
being different from one another, being separate.
And so we name them to distinguish them from one another.
After all, how else can we talk about them?

We feel what we call the passage of time.
We believe yesterday is past, the future is not yet here,
and the present is a transitory moment between one and the other.

However, we create trouble for ourselves because
      we don't stop there.
We see different things as good and bad; we judge them.
We look backwards in time and judge things in the past
      –that's where regret comes from.
We look forward in time and judge things in the future
      –that's where worry and fear come from.
And our judgments affect what we do.
So many different things at different points in time.
No wonder there can be discord, shadows, and confusion.

But what if what we see and what we feel are not all there is?
What if there's more than this world of things
      and the passage of time?
What if they are simply different manifestations
of Oneness/Wholeness? What if the only moment is now?

If that is true, then there's no such thing as good and bad.
There's no judgment. No regret. No fear.
No discord. No shadows. No confusion.

Just harmony, light, and peace.
What if that world is here right now?
What if we're here just to contribute to the harmony?

The previous observation, "What If," wondered, What if our everyday experience of life is an illusion caused by seeing ourselves as separate from everything we observe. It ended by wondering, "What if we simply lived in the Oneness?" This observation explores what happens when we don't live in the Oneness, as it were—when we ignore this question and instead live as though the illusion is real. Does it really make any difference? Let's find out.

Our everyday experience tells us there are countless things out there. It also tells us that today is about to become yesterday and that tomorrow will become today. And so it seems we live surrounded by things and are swept along in "the passage of time." What do we do about that?

Well, for a start, what we do is name everything we can lay our eyes on so we can distinguish different things from one another. As this observation reminds us, "After all, how else can we talk about them?" And we certainly love to talk. As for the passage of time, we typically think of the present moment as a "transitory moment" between the past and the future. It is also a convenient opportunity to shape whatever is around us today into the way we would like it to be tomorrow. We have a name for that too; it is called "satisfying desires."

This observation then notes, "However, we create trouble for ourselves because we don't stop there." The *Tao Te Ching* points to the same danger. "If you close your mind in judgments and traffic with desires, your heart will be troubled" (chapter 52). So, what is causing the trouble? The answer, in a word, is judgment—specifically our judgment. The *Tao Te Ching* notes this too. "When people see some things as beautiful, other things become ugly. When people see some things as good, other things become bad" (chapter 2). This means that when we are the people doing the judging, we are where the trouble comes from.

What's more, when we combine judging with looking into the past and the future, we get whole new categories of trouble. "We look backwards in time and judge things in the past—that's where regret comes from. We look forward in time and judge things in the future—that's where worry and fear come from." So now we have created both regret and worry. What happens next is that we start to fear our creations and let them directly affect what we do. In other words, we do not stop at naming things; we go on to create all sorts of trouble for ourselves. "No wonder there can be discord, shadows, and confusion."

In all fairness, it's important to note that we can also look forward with joyful anticipation, and we can look back on the past with fond memories. So, it's not all doom and gloom every time we leave the present moment. The point is that regret, worry, and fear can exist only when we dwell in the past or the future. They cannot exist anywhere else.

The previous observation looked at how making all these distinctions creates the world of "manifestations" that we live in. We saw how, while they all seem real enough to us at the time, none of them is what the *Tao Te Ching* calls "eternally real." They are all temporary; they come and they go. They are no more than "different manifestations of Oneness/Wholeness." So, what happens if we let them all go? Things, judgments, the passage of time, all of it—what if we just let it all go? What are we left with?

One way to work out the answer is by elimination. We are left with "no judgment. No regret. No fear." That is not a bad start. How about "no discord. No shadows. No confusion." It is getting better. Note how we are following where the Master leads us. "The Master leads by emptying people's minds. . . . He helps people lose everything they know, everything they desire, and creates confusion in those who think that they know" (chapter 3). We can tell we are following successfully because at this point "confusion" is likely a pretty good description of how we feel!

So, what happens when our mind is finally empty? The answer is that the moment we stop separating and judging, we suddenly discover there is "no such thing as good and bad." That means discord, shadows, and confusion disappear. (They were actually never there in the first place—we created them.) What is left is Oneness/Wholeness and nothing else. If we have to put words around it then we might try words like "harmony, light, and peace." But, if you think about, every word represents a thought. Do we need the words?

How often we live surrounded by things and swept along in "the passage of time." As long as we look at everything from our perspective, it is indeed all very real. Or perhaps we should say it is as real as anything temporary can be. (After all, we know things come and go—and none of them seems to be here for very long, ourselves included.) Nonetheless, we can live successfully enough in this world of "manifestations" acting as if it is real. We can chase after our desires, even satisfy them sometimes—at least until some new desire springs up to replace the last one. We can also get used to living with fear, regret, worry—or what this observation calls discord, shadows, and confusion. We can get used to living with all of that if we choose to.

But have you ever wondered whether it needs to be this way? Might it appear to be this way only because of our perspective? Might we be the ones who make it so? What would happen if we stopped seeing ourselves as separate and somehow at the center of it all?

This chapter's observation reminds us we can let go of our perspective any time we choose. Maybe we don't have to strive to be anywhere other than where we are right now. If the only thing that is eternally real is Oneness/Wholeness, then the good news is that we are already home. If we are already home, then what are we doing here with our lifetime? "What if we're here just to contribute to the harmony?" Perhaps it's as simple as that.

34

INSIDE EVERY MOMENT

Inside every moment is a song.
Inside every moment is light.
When you fill the moment with your self,
you stifle the song and dim the light.

Let go of your self and listen and watch.
The song is inside you. So sing it.
The light is inside you. So let it shine.

Sing the song. Embody the light.
Become the song. Become the light.
Be the song. Be the light.

Be inside the moment.
Become the moment.
Be the moment.

Be.

This observation is about song and light. We all know what it feels like when our days are harmonious and full of light. Our lives feel effortless and joyful. But we also know what it feels like when our days are full of discord and struggle and the light is dim. On very dark days, it can even feel like the light goes out. When this happens, we ask: Where is the song, where is the light? This observation suggests the answer is that they are "inside every moment." In other words, they are there all the time. How can that possibly be true? This observation explores an answer.

Most of the time we tend not to be open to whatever is in the moment. Instead, we tend to fill it with whatever we want. In other words, whatever we "want" suddenly becomes what the moment is full of. (Or rather, the lack of whatever we want is what the moment becomes full of.) So, unless the moment happens to already be one of harmony and joy, we can be sure of one thing—it will become full of something that it is not. Instead of reality, we will have filled the moment with one of our wants or desires. To do that is to fill it with our self. And what happens? "When you fill the moment with your self, you stifle the song and dim the light." That is where discord comes from. That is how the light dims.

It is natural to want to be fulfilled, to want to experience harmony and light. But when we reach for these things or try to grasp them, it seems we lose them every time. The *Tao Te Ching* reminds us, "He who tries to shine dims his own light" (chapter 24). We may think: Yes, but how can we succeed without trying? The answer is easy to say but hard to do. The answer is simply to let go. This is what the Master does. "Because she has let go of herself, she is perfectly fulfilled" (chapter 7). It is the trying that takes up the space inside the moment. When we try, it is our self that fills the moment with our trying.

All we need for the light to shine is to get our self out of the way. "The Master, by residing in the Tao, sets an example for all beings. Because he doesn't display himself, people can see his light" (chapter 22). The reason he succeeds is that he is not trying. Trying to achieve the goal of living in the light is precisely what is blocking the light. "Because he has no goal in mind, everything he does succeeds" (chapter 22). Suppose we follow the Master's example and let go of our self? What will be inside the moment if we are not there? The answer is everything—harmony, light, joy, fulfillment—everything we could possibly want, if only we could let go of wanting it!

Every time we want the moment to be anything other than what it is, we are outside the moment looking in. When we let go of our self, suddenly we are inside the moment, our wants disappear, and we discover that the moment is actually perfect just the way it is. "When you realize there is nothing lacking, the whole world belongs to you" (chapter 44). The moment itself needs no improvement. What's more, we are fully present in it. No part of us is off somewhere else wanting things to be different.

So, when we let this happen, what is our response? What do we do now? I think the answer is to let our self become part of the expression of the moment. "The song is inside you. So sing it. The light is inside you. So let it shine." The singing and the shining are the expression. In fact, everything around you is part of the expression of the moment, including you—the situation, the people, everything, all of it. "Thus the Master is available to all people and doesn't reject anyone. He is ready to use all situations and doesn't waste anything. This is called embodying the light" (chapter 27).

When you sing the song and embody the light, what happens is that "you" disappear. You become the song; you become the light. That is why this observation encourages us, "Be the song. Be the light." With each moment, the place to be is not on the outside looking in. The place to be is inside the moment—not looking anywhere. When we become the moment, it becomes who we are. When that happens, all that is left is "being." And that, it turns out, is everything.

How often we live outside the moment looking in. We become observers separated from what we are observing, and we typically make all sorts of judgments. Our language speaks for us. We label things not merely as preferable or less so, but often as good or bad. And we judge not only things but also other people, and we judge ourselves as well. We can develop countless ways in which the moment "should be" something other than what it is.

This is not to say that every moment is easy and harmonious. Although this observation says, "Inside every moment is a song," it would be more accurate to say that every moment is what it is. What happens is that we tend to complicate it when we look at it from the outside. To be centered in the moment is to forget our self and our judgments and to be centered in the Tao. "She who is centered in the Tao can go where she wishes, without danger. She perceives the universal harmony, even amid great pain, because she has found peace in her heart" (chapter 35).

This chapter's observation reminds us that there is no greater song than universal harmony.

35
YOU ARE NOT ALONE

You are a newcomer.
You don't recognize this place and you don't like it.
You look around and nothing is familiar.
Everything is new. You didn't choose this.
You don't know why you're here.
You feel lost and alone.

So listen up, because some things matter and some things don't.
It doesn't matter that you didn't choose this
and that you don't recognize where you are.
You're simply someplace you haven't been before.

The territory is unfamiliar but it is not uncharted.
So you are not lost.
Others are here but you simply haven't met them yet.
So you are not alone.

Charts provide guidance, so open your mind and study them.
People provide support, so open your arms and accept it.
One day, sooner than you think, it will be your turn
to update the charts and support the next newcomer.

In the meantime, accept our welcome.
What matters is that you're here now.
And you are not alone.

Sometimes we have good days, and sometimes we have bad days. Some days are so profoundly confusing we wonder what on earth we are doing here. It can even feel like we have woken up in the wrong place and don't recognize where we are. If we are young, we may see a long road ahead of us and wonder why we are here and what our life is all about. This observation addresses days like these.

Before we start, it is worth remembering that when we refer to good and bad days, we are the ones who attach these labels. "Good" and "bad" are no more than convenient ways of stating our preferences. It would be more accurate to say, "Relative to the good days I have experienced, today is a bad day," but that's certainly not very convenient. Besides, what matters more is that the words we use reflect how we feel. For us, the world is as we see it. And sometimes, on a bad day, what we feel is lost and alone.

At times like this, we think no one else can possibly understand how we feel. But then we meet someone who does seem to understand. We can tell they understand because the words they use make it seem as though they are reading our minds. They say things like, "You don't know why you're here. You feel lost and alone." Yes, we think, that's exactly right; that's exactly how I feel. These people are worth listening to. This observation captures the words one of them is saying.

Note that the newcomer who is addressed in this observation is having more than a bad day. He or she is wondering what they are doing here at all, and they are not liking the experience. They are caught up in what the *Tao Te Ching* refers to as "the turmoil of beings" and "stumbling in confusion and sorrow." The words spoken to them, however, would likely not have come from the Master in the *Tao Te Ching*. This is for one simple reason: the Master never tells people what to do. The most he does, I think, is make neutral observations as to what follows from the choices we make—especially when we make the mistake of thinking we have no choice.

So, when this observation says, "Listen up, because some things matter and some things don't," we are hearing harsher words than the Master would use. However, the words certainly get our attention. What follows is a quick list of things that don't matter, all of which summarize the way the newcomer is feeling. For a moment, imagine yourself as the newcomer. You are told that the fact that you didn't choose what you're experiencing right now doesn't matter. The fact that you don't recognize where you are doesn't matter. Regardless of how you feel, apparently neither of these matters. Instead, you are told, "You're simply someplace you haven't been before." Well, yes, that is also true. But here's why this matters: it sidesteps the list completely.

You may feel lost because the territory is unfamiliar, but you are told it is not uncharted. This means you are not in fact lost, regardless of how you feel. You may feel alone, but you are told there are people here whom you haven't met. This means you are not in fact alone, regardless of how you feel. These facts matter more than what you feel. Why? Because they point to what you can do. "Charts provide guidance, so open your mind and study them. People provide support, so open your arms and accept it."

The *Tao Te Ching* goes further when it suggests, "Empty your mind of all thoughts. Let your heart be at peace. Watch the turmoil of beings, but contemplate their return. Each separate being in the universe returns to the common source. Returning to the source is serenity" (chapter 16). "If you don't realize the source, you stumble in confusion and sorrow" (chapter 16). But what does the "source" have to do with looking at charts and accepting support from others?

I think the connection is as follows: The "source" is the one place where we are not lost and alone. And the source is everywhere, whether we realize it or not. "The great Tao flows everywhere. All things are born from it" (chapter 34). And, when we are lost, the great Tao is still there. It is in the charts, if only we let ourselves be guided. It is in the people who could support us, if only we would let them. Our part is simpler than we think. Our part is to be open and respond. The moment we are open, we are no longer lost. It is like waking from a dream. We become aware of what matters and what doesn't matter.

In that moment of waking, we are also no longer newcomers. However, we can recognize newcomers when we see them. We know what it feels like to be inside their skin. Now it is our turn to welcome them and support them. Now it is our turn to say things like "What matters is that you're here now. And you are not alone."

How often we have a tough time accepting the experience of our lives. Days can be good or bad or full of light or darkness, not to mention every shade of grey in between. And the darkest days are certainly those when we feel lost and alone. On those days even the most crowded city street can feel like the loneliest place on earth.

Have you ever wondered about the millions of lives that have been lived over the centuries? Or the millions of lives that are being lived right now? Our darkest day has likely been lived millions of times by other people. But that is little consolation. After all, it is our darkest day—not anyone else's. But what if all it takes is for someone to recognize what is going on? What if all it takes is for someone to take you aside and remind you, hopefully with compassion, that some things matter and some things don't? That what matters is that you are here right now and that you are not alone.

This chapter's observation reminds us that we can be the ones reaching out. We can be the ones who remind others. We can be the ones who say, "Accept our welcome." At the end of the day, none of us is alone. "The Tao gives birth to all beings, nourishes them, maintains them, cares for them, comforts them, protects them, takes them back to itself" (chapter 51). We are all in good hands. None of us is ever alone.

36
NO OTHER WAY

Right now, in this moment,
you are in exactly the right place
at exactly the right time.

And the only way you could have arrived
is exactly the way you came.
There is no other way.

Accept everything. Regret nothing.

Looking back briefly to learn is fine
because it may change how you respond in the future.
But looking back to regret is a waste of time.

Looking forward briefly to plan is fine
because it may influence what you do.
But looking forward in fear or worry is another waste of time.

Regret, fear, worry . . . they accomplish nothing.
They make no difference.
All they leave is a bitter taste.

The only thing that matters
is that you are right here, right now.
And the only way you could have arrived
is exactly the way you came.

There is no other way.

The previous observation, "You Are Not Alone," contained words spoken to a newcomer who was not sure what he or she was doing here. It ended by reassuring them they were neither lost nor alone. This observation goes further and suggests there is actually no way they could have arrived at the present moment other than the way they came. Does this matter? Yes, I think it does. This observation explores why.

It seems to be human nature to ask "What if?" questions. What if something else had happened in the past? If it had, then how would the present moment have turned out differently? What if something unforeseen happens in the future? In case it does, should I be using the present moment to somehow avert it or prepare for it? These are natural questions to ask, and it would make little sense to completely ignore them. Failing to learn from past experience would be to invite difficult situations that could be avoided. Failing to look ahead would be to miss opportunities where one's actions could make a useful difference.

Clearly there are upsides to asking "What if?" questions. However, there is also a large downside. The downside is that we don't know when to stop. If we're not careful, we can quickly create so much mud in front of our eyes that we no longer see clearly. This is the mud the *Tao Te Ching* refers to in the lines "Do you have the patience to wait till your mud settles and the water is clear? Can you remain unmoving till the right action arises by itself?" (chapter 15). Much of the time, our honest answer to the question as to whether we can "remain unmoving" would be "No, we can't." What's worse, our lack of patience stirs up even more mud. So, when we do this, what is it that we are failing to understand?

Let's stand back for a moment. Everything we do, or do not do, has consequences that influence our experience of life. We can seldom entirely control the outcome of our actions, but we are nonetheless responsible for what we do. And so we discover that our experience of life depends only partly on what we do; the rest is simply not up to us. This is neither good nor bad—it's just the way it is.

So, let's look at where we are right now in the present moment. How did we get here? The answer lies in the particular combination of past moments that we experienced and the things we did at the time. Could we control all of it? No. Are we responsible for all of it? No. We are responsible only for what we did or didn't do—that's all. But it was this particular combination of past moments, whatever it was, that brought us to exactly where we are in this present moment. Again, this is neither good nor bad—it's just the way it is. I think this is what we fail to understand.

What creates mud is thinking the present moment should be anything other than what it is. This amounts to asserting our will and thereby entering what the *Tao Te Ching* calls the illusion. This is what the Master is aware of. "He has no will of his own. He dwells in reality, and lets all illusions go" (chapter 38). If the Master were to have a "will of his own" (which he doesn't), then it would be to hold on to his personal version of what he thinks reality should be. But the Master is aware this would be an illusion. This is the illusion he lets go of. Actually, he lets go by never holding on to it in the first place.

This does not mean time spent in the past and future is always wasted. It depends on how long we spend there. "Looking back briefly to learn is fine" and "looking forward briefly to plan is fine," but the emphasis is on the word "briefly." It is when we dwell in the past and the future that regret, fear, and worry creep in. This is what happens when we don't know when to stop. This is the downside showing itself. "Regret, fear, worry . . . they accomplish nothing."

In the words of this observation, "The only thing that matters is that you are here right now." So, instead of letting the past and the future distract us for longer than is useful, the suggestion is that we accept that "right now, in this moment, you are in exactly the right place at exactly the right time." And before we wonder how we got here, we are reminded, "And the only way you could have arrived is exactly the way you came. There is no other way."

How often we look back and regret. How often we look forward and worry. How often we create illusions about how our experience of life would be so much better if only something else had happened. We ask ourselves: How is it that we ended up here when this "something else" would have been so much better?

Have you ever thought how we can always ask ourselves this question, regardless of what the present moment may be? The present moment could be perfect just the way it is, and we could still imagine some other sequence of events that would have resulted in our ending up somewhere else.

Here's a good way to nip this question in the bud: simply notice the moment we start wondering how we got here. Unless we're making a brief trip into the past to learn then why are we lingering there? Imagining how things might have turned out differently makes about as much sense as looking in the rearview mirror trying to rearrange what has already happened, thinking that doing so will somehow cause us to be in a different place in the present. It simply doesn't work that way. If we think it does, we're kidding ourselves.

This chapter's observation reminds us there is only one way we could have arrived where we are right now—and that is exactly the way we came. If we look back, then this observation reminds us to do so briefly. The reason this matters is that every moment spent dwelling in the past is a moment not spent being alive in the present. The only difference you can make is through what you do in this present moment, right here, right now. What's more, there is "no other way" to make a difference.

37
THERE IS NO SOMEWHERE ELSE

You do not have to be here.
You are free to go elsewhere.
And often you do.

Sometimes you take a trip into the future.
"It would be so much better if . . . ," you think.
And away you go into something, anything,
other than what is here right now.

Sometimes you take a trip into the past.
"I should have . . . . If only . . . ," you think.
And away you go again.

The future, the past, anywhere but the present moment
is whatever you think it is.
If you don't like it, just think differently, and it is so.
If you don't like where you are,
you can always go somewhere else.

Countless other places are yours to think up.
And you can dwell in them as long as you like.
But all of them are illusions.

Reality is what is here right now.
To dwell here, you need do only one thing.
Let go of liking and disliking.

Countless illusions. Only one reality.
There is no somewhere else.

We've likely all heard the phrase "here and now is all there is." We may also have thought it to be true in some abstract sense. Interesting perhaps, but somehow irrelevant to whatever we're doing, wherever we happen to be at the time. This is the point this observation explores. In other words, where exactly are we when we are having these thoughts? The answer is that we are "somewhere else." And there is nothing abstract or irrelevant about that.

The first lines note our freedom in this respect. "You do not have to be here. You are free to go elsewhere. And often you do." However, it seems every time we go elsewhere, we can easily become unaware of what we just did. The reason for this is that awareness lies in only one place—the present moment. When we are aware, we are right here, right now. If "here and now is all there is," then, whenever we go somewhere else, we enter an illusion.

The *Tao Te Ching* makes many references to this illusion. To believe you can really go somewhere else is to be distracted by the superficial. For example, "Therefore the Master concerns himself with the depths and not the surface, with the fruit and not the flower. . . . He dwells in reality, and lets all illusions go" (chapter 38). Let's dig a little deeper.

Whenever we leave the here and now, there are only two places we can go: either forward into the future or backwards into the past. These are the only types of "somewhere else" available to us. This observation suggests that both are illusions because you can play with them, and alter them, as much as you like. "If you don't like it, just think differently, and it is so. If you don't like where you are, you can always go somewhere else." If you don't like this flower, then here is another flower, and another. Within each of the two types of "somewhere else" we are limited only by our imagination. What's more, we can do this for as long as we want.

In all this, I think the key word is "like." And it is a problem because it represents a preference, an opinion. "When people see some things as good, other things become bad" (chapter 2). How we see things would not be a problem if it weren't for the fact that it becomes the basis for how we act in the world. When we don't like whatever we are experiencing right now, we tend to imagine a "better version" in the future and then strive to bring it into the present by trying to make it so. At other times, we look backwards and imagine a better version that could have existed had something different happened in the past. We think thoughts that start with "I should have . . ." or "If only . . . ."

Unless we are learning from it, contemplating a different past is perhaps more pointless than imagining a different future, because there's nothing we can do to alter the past. Our present actions have at least the potential to alter the future. In this respect, imagining future actions is less pointless than contemplating past ones, because the future hasn't happened yet—so there may be something we can do about it. Nonetheless, what matters is that there is no limit to what we can imagine. None of it is real, yet we can easily hold on to it. When we do so, we can end up dwelling there a lot of the time. "Countless other places are yours to think up. And you can dwell in them as long as you like. But all of them are illusions."

This is exactly what the Master is aware of. "The Master gives himself up to whatever the moment brings. He knows that he is going to die, and he has nothing left to hold on to: no illusions in his mind, no resistances in his body. He doesn't think about his actions; they flow from the core of his being" (chapter 50). The important point is that the Master's actions do not flow from liking or disliking whatever is here right now—these would be the "illusions in his mind." So, this is exactly what he does not "think about," what he does not "hold on to." Why? Because both liking and disliking are at the root of the desire to be somewhere else. "Reality is what is here right now. To dwell here, you need do only one thing. Let go of the liking and disliking." Once you do that, everything else flows.

How often we would like to be anywhere other than where we are right now—as long as it is a better place, of course. And there is the problem, the word "better." It is the thin end of the wedge that ends in "good" and "bad" that then directs our actions. If we think it a good place, then we strive for it. If we think it a bad place, then we try to avoid it. In both cases, "somewhere else" is where we are trying to be.

What if the peace and serenity we seek has been under our feet all the time? What if there is nowhere else we need to go? What if we are already there? "Thus the Master travels all day without leaving home. However splendid the views, she stays serenely in herself" (chapter 26). There may be countless splendid views out there, but the moment you try to travel to them, "if you let restlessness move you, you lose touch with who you are" (chapter 26). Peace and serenity are the opposite of restlessness, and they come from being in touch with who you are, which comes from being here and now. Peace and serenity never come from being somewhere else.

This chapter's observation reminds us there is no limit to the amount of traveling we may choose to do. However, all of it takes us in the wrong direction, as it were. "Countless illusions. Only one reality. There is no somewhere else."

38
EACH OF US IS THE UNIVERSE

Each of us is the universe aware of itself
as localized in space and time—at least for the time being.
We are temporary units of localized awareness.
Sounds a bit humbling, doesn't it?

In space, we exist on what we call planet Earth.
In time, we exist for what we call one human lifetime.
While we are here, each of us seems separate,
both from one another and from the universe.
We call these separate units our selves.

Outside space and time, our selves do not exist.
They exist only for the time being,
which comes to an end soon enough.
Death is simply an end to the self as we know it.
What then? Who knows?
Besides, when there is no self, who is there to do the knowing?

Outside space and time there is no here and there,
no yesterday and no tomorrow.
From inside, we could call it an eternal now.
But from outside, the words "now" and "eternal" make no sense.
No space and no time mean no separation.
Just the Oneness/Wholeness of the universe.
Just Oneness.

But, in the meantime, we are inside.
So space and time seem real for us. Separation seems real.
We are conscious of our separate self. We are self-conscious.
We cannot return to yesterday. We have to wait for tomorrow.

And we don't know how many tomorrows each of us will have.
It is all real enough for the time being.
So what are we doing here?

In our self-consciousness, we have a choice
as to how we live our temporary lives.
We can live as though what seems real is all there is
or we can live in awareness of Oneness/Wholeness.
Our choice matters because it causes different things to unfold.
And these different things are real enough for the time being.

When we live centered in our self, we live as though
      separation is real.
We believe in yours and mine, in space and time,
that tomorrow I can amass more than I had yesterday,
that differences matter. We increase the separation
and our actions tend to create conflict and confusion.

When we let our self go, we live centered in Oneness.
Everything we do springs from Oneness.
Differences do not matter.
Yours, mine, more, less, yesterday, tomorrow
- none of it matters. We recognize the unity
and our actions create peace and serenity.

So let us choose consciously. Our time here is limited.
Consciousness of our separate self will soon end.
In the meantime, all that matters is
how we spend what we call time
in the place that we call here.

Each of us is the universe aware of itself.
Which shall we choose? Separation or unity?
What shall we create today?

So, I'm a temporary unit of localized awareness, am I? Well, I am not sure I feel humbled but I certainly don't feel flattered. Instead, I'm wondering where this observation will take me and whether or not I will enjoy the ride. This observation takes us outside ourselves and asks the question, What is there when we are not? And the surprising answer is everything, or the universe, or whatever you want to call it.

How do we get there from here? The short answer is, we are there all the time whether we realize it or not—and most of the time we don't. Why? Because our self gets in the way. Instead of being aware of the universe we tend to be aware of our self. This has consequences for what we experience and for how we live our lives. This observation explores these consequences.

As every human being knows, space and time seem very real. Different places occupy different positions in space, and we cannot be in two places at the same time. Similarly, time flows forward. We cannot relive yesterday or prevent tomorrow from coming, or make it come any sooner than it's going to come anyway. So, when we ask, What is this place, and for how much time are we here? The simple answer is that we are on planet Earth, and we are each here for the length of one human lifetime. That's just the way it is. Or perhaps we should be a little humbler and say that this is about as much as we can easily understand from our perspective.

But what about a perspective that is broader than ours? Is there a reality that might exist outside space and time? If so, what might that look like? Clearly, it would look like nothing we can relate to as long as our view is from inside our self. This means the only way to explore this reality is by seeing what happens when we let ourselves go.

Here are some words that describe where we are headed: "There was something formless and perfect before the universe was born. It is serene. Empty. Solitary. Unchanging. Infinite. Eternally present. It is the mother of the universe. For lack of a better name, I call it the Tao. It flows through all things, inside and outside, and returns to the origin of all things" (chapter 25).

It is hard to relate to what Lao Tzu is talking about, isn't it? This is because words no longer work very well. This is why he says, "For lack of a better name . . . ." And he is quite right; we don't have words for it. For a start, how can something exist before the universe was born? Before and after are time-bound concepts. So he takes another shot at it. "Since before time and space were, the Tao is. It is beyond *is* and *is not*" (chapter 21). That seems like a better shot, but we still cannot relate to it because it doesn't make what we call sense.

The trouble is, we lack words for anything that is beyond words. "Outside space and time, there is no here and there, no yesterday and no tomorrow. From inside, we could call it an eternal now. But from the outside, the words 'now' and 'eternal' make no sense." Similarly, what is there when there are no distinctions in space? The answer is, everything and no thing.

So where are we now? Well, for now we live on the inside, where we see things as separate. We have become used to this, and we give different things different names so we can make distinctions between them. We have no problem with *is* and *is not*. For example, something either *is* or *is not* ours. We can chase after something we don't have yet and make it ours. But this is where it gets interesting. Not-having-something-yet increases our experience of time. Today we don't have something, tomorrow we do. Yesterday we had a desire, today it is fulfilled. That seems very real to us. So our experience of time feels very real.

How does that compare with the Tao? "The Tao is infinite, eternal. Why is it eternal? It was never born; thus it can never die. Why is it infinite? It has no desires for itself; thus it is present for all beings" (chapter 7). So, is it desire that creates our experience of time? We might think that even if we desired nothing, we would still have to wait for the sun to rise tomorrow. But the very notion of "waiting" is on this side of "*is* and *is not*" and so creates the experience of time. (We would be waiting for the sun to rise because it *is not* tomorrow.) In the present moment, there is no tomorrow.

If we dwell in the moment, we are "present for all beings." If we dwell anywhere else, we are simply not present. Some part of us is somewhere else, looking back at yesterday or wondering about tomorrow's sunrise. When we are fully present our self disappears and, when that happens, time ceases to exist. In the moment itself, there is only "now"—there is only the moment and no thing else, not even our self.

Does all this make a difference? The short answer is yes. Why? Because we can choose to let go of our self any time we want. The moment we do, there are no more distinctions, nothing is separate any more. There is everything and no thing. Everything is one. And here is the difference. "When we let our self go, we live centered in Oneness.... We recognize the unity and our actions create peace and serenity." "When we live centered in our self.... We increase the separation and our actions tend to create conflict and confusion." This is quite a difference, isn't it?

Lao Tzu's Master is aware of this. "She is detached from all things; that is why she is one with them. Because she has let go of herself, she is perfectly fulfilled" (chapter 7). The message is clear. Fulfillment comes from letting go of our self, thereby living fully in the present moment, and thereby also being at one with everything.

How often we live as though our experience in this world of space and time is all there is. How often we live not only centered in our self but as though we have no choice about it. When Lao Tzu's Master lives "detached from all things," we may wonder: Is she living in the same world as ours? What if the answer is yes? Have you ever thought of yourself as a temporary fragment of the universe being aware of itself? It's not your average, everyday thought, is it? But what if it's true? Or, more to the point, what if you lived *as though* it were true? It is in this respect that "each of us is the universe."

This chapter's observation reminds us that it matters whether or not we let go of our self. If we hold on, we become more likely to create conflict and confusion. If we let go, we are more likely to create peace and serenity. We experience what we create—and what we create is a choice. "So let us choose consciously.... What shall we create today?"

PART 2

A MAP

This part of the book is the map. If you recall the preface, it is, strictly speaking, "*a* map." This is because other maps are also possible. This is no more than one mapmaker's idea of where you have been. But before we look at it, let me say a bit about how this map came to be made.

Lao Tzu's *Tao Te Ching* is not a long book. It consists of 81 brief chapters, some of them very brief. As such, it needs no summarizing. The book stands quite firmly on its own feet. Nonetheless, if we were to summarize the key ideas, then what would that look like? This map is an attempt to answer this question.

Why make this attempt? In short, to satisfy curiosity. Three questions spring to my curious mind. First, if we think of each key idea as a building block, then how many building blocks does it take to capture the essence of the *Tao Te Ching*? Second, in what sequence should the blocks be laid so they stack neatly and support one another? Third, for me, the essence of Lao Tzu's book is how it shows the differences between being centered in the Tao and being centered in our self. If this is true, then what would a table of these differences look like?

I think the answer to the first question is sixteen. The answer to the second question is the sequence in which the key ideas are listed below. The answer to the third question is shown in a table with 33 rows and two columns representing being centered in our self versus being centered in the Tao. These three elements are what the "map" consists of. Like all maps, it is an abstraction. But I think every part of the journey we have taken in the first part of this book fits somewhere on it.

I hope you enjoy this map of where I think our journey has taken us. On the other hand, if you're starting this book by reading this map first, then I hope you enjoy the journey you're about to undertake and the sights you will see along the way.

List of Key Ideas

1. **The Tao.** There is only one reality. It is Oneness/Wholeness. "It is serene. Empty. Solitary. Unchanging. Infinite. Eternally present. It is the mother of the universe. For lack of a better name, I call it the Tao" (*Tao Te Ching*, chapter 25).

2. **The self.** In this human life we experience the self. The self sees itself as separate and apart from the reality of Oneness/Wholeness. In reality, of course, the self is not separate and apart (see No.1)—but it thinks it is. We not only experience our self; we also think we *are* our self.

3. **Thought.** The self is the origin of all thoughts.

4. **Confusion.** Thinking that we are separate and apart invariably brings confusion. This is because any thought of separateness does not align with reality (see No.1).

5. **The search.** This confusion causes us to experience a feeling of being lonely and lost and trying to find our way home. The self does not see itself as the origin of this confusion. It thinks the confusion lies in the "outside world." The self wants to return home, not realizing that it is already there.

6. **Desire.** Not seeing and not accepting the "outside world" as it is, the self desires a better version of reality in which it thinks it will experience less confusion. The self directs us to take action to rearrange reality into its idea of what reality should be. Our actions have consequences. Sometimes we succeed in fulfilling our desires, at least for a while. Sometimes our actions have unintended side effects. Other times we fail. Trying to force-fit reality into our idea of what it should be invariably brings more confusion and often stress and frustration. Sadly, we often think the solution is to try harder.

7. **The illusion.** We are home the moment we no longer take direction from the self. When we let our self go, we discover that we never left home. We were there all along. But the illusion is powerful because the self takes itself very seriously.

8. **The continuous unfolding of Oneness/Wholeness.** "In harmony with the Tao, the sky is clear and spacious, the earth is solid and full, all creatures flourish together, content with the way they are, endlessly repeating themselves, endlessly renewed" (chapter 39). This is neither right nor wrong. It's just the way it is. This is what's going on regardless of what we think about it.

9. **Our role in the unfolding.** We each have a unique part to play in the unfolding. We each have a unique song to sing in harmony with the music all around us. When we sing in harmony, we experience peace and serenity. When we don't, we often experience confusion and stress.

10. **The choice.** During this human lifetime we have a choice. We can be centered in the Tao or centered in our self. At all times we are centered in one of these two places whether we are aware of it or not.

The *Tao Te Ching* describes being centered in the Tao as being at the center of the circle. "The Master sees things as they are, without trying to control them. She lets them go their own way, and resides at the center of the circle" (chapter 29). "Just stay at the center of the circle and let all things take their course" (chapter 19). The next two building blocks summarize our experience of being centered in our self (the edge of the circle) as opposed to being centered in the Tao (the center of the circle).

11. **Centered in our self**
- We hear nothing but the noise of our own thoughts.
- Our actions spring from desire and desire creates expectation.
- At best, our expectations will be met. We experience moments of fleeting satisfaction.
- At worst, we experience disappointment.

- What's more, these feelings come and go as new thoughts and desires spring up to pull us this way and that.
- We feel separate and apart as we try to stand alone.
- We live in various forms of confusion and stress.
- We do not accept reality just the way it is. Our desire is for it to be different.
- We use our actions to try to rearrange reality to match our desires.
- We tend to look to the past with regret or blame.
- We tend to look to the future with worry or fear.
- We often live not in the present moment.
- We are at the edge of the circle.

12. Centered in the Tao

- The noise of our thoughts stops.
- We become aware of the Tao continuously unfolding in endless cycles of expression and renewal.
- Desire and expectation fall away.
- We hear harmony all around us.
- Our actions spring from the Tao.
- At best, we experience pure joy as we add our unique notes to the music.
- At worst, we are carried by the Tao because no thoughts and desires pull us this way and that.
- Either way, we live in peace and serenity.
- These feelings do not come and go, as there are no fleeting moments in the Tao. It always was and always will be. It is going nowhere. It simply is.
- We do not feel separate and apart. We do not feel alone. (We never were, even when we thought we were.)
- We accept reality exactly the way it is without desiring that it be any different.
- We use our actions to contribute to the harmony.
- We look to the past only to learn a little if we can.
- We look to the future only to plan a little if we can.
- We are aware that the present moment is all there is.
- We are at the center of the circle.

13. **We are born asleep and are here to wake up.** Centered in ourselves it is as though we are asleep. We miss experiencing reality as it is because we see it only in terms of what we want it to be. When we do this, we live inside the illusion. Centered in the Tao we are awake. We live in reality, aware of being part of the Oneness/Wholeness. Strictly speaking, even being a "part" is a thought because Oneness/Wholeness can have no parts—it just is. Thus we are here to awaken to the fact that we actually *are* the Oneness/Wholeness, along with everything else that we see as separate. In reality, none of it is separate. As Thich Nhat Hanh says, "We are here to awaken from the illusion of our separateness."

The next three building blocks are a contribution of mine, because they are not as obviously present in the *Tao Te Ching* as the previous ones. Nonetheless, they are written in the same spirit and, I believe, can be stacked on top of the other key ideas to round out the view we see when we stand on top.

14. **Once awake, we are here to sing.** What unique talents have we been born with? How can we discover and develop them? How can we add to the harmony? How can we use our actions to make a positive difference in the world around us before we die? This is what each human life is all about. This is why we are here. Life is short.

15. **It is not complicated.** It is only our self that would have us think so. Living a human life is simple in principle but difficult in practice. And the reason it is difficult is that we have to deal with our self and our thoughts.

16. **Treat thoughts as servants, not as masters.** Is thought good for anything, or does it always get in the way? Yes, thought is good for many things. Thought has its place and time, just not everywhere and not all of the time. This is why thought needs to be managed and treated as no more than a useful tool.

We can use thought to build knowledge. We can use knowledge to discover aspects of the world around us. We can apply our knowledge to control aspects of the world. Science, art, technology, medicine—all the fields of human study are the result of thought. They are all fine and useful; but thought is still no more than a tool.

All is well as long as we are master, treat thought as our servant, and tell it what to do. The confusion starts when the roles are reversed and thought becomes our master and tells us what to do. If we are not careful, this can happen in an instant without our being aware of it. This is why dwelling in the Tao, as opposed to in our own thoughts, is something to practice with every moment of every day.

Table of Differences

The table below summarizes 33 differences between living centered in the self and living centered in the Tao. It includes Key Ideas 11 and 12 from the previous list, and adds a few more.

CENTERED IN THE SELF	**CENTERED IN THE TAO**

View of world

Sees world as full of separate forms	Sees only Oneness/Wholeness, with all forms being different manifestations of the One. "Every being in the universe is an expression of the Tao" (chapter 51)
Believes that what we can see is all there is (i.e., that the temporary illusion is real and is the only reality there is)	Believes there is only one eternal reality (which includes the temporary illusion), but we cannot see it—although we can live in awareness of it

View of self

Sees self as separate and apart. Believes in its own identity.	Sees self as part of the Tao just like everything else (and not even a "part")
Self is "outer" self or self-image or ego	Self is "inner" self already in harmony with the Tao, just waiting to be expressed (and not even an "inner self" because this implies separateness)
Seeks approval of others for self-validation, self-esteem	Opinion of others is irrelevant, self-validation is not needed
Seeks to preserve self at all costs	Lets the self go
Allows thought to be master	Sees thought as a useful servant

What you hear

Noise of your own thoughts	Silence, then harmony everywhere

Desire

Desire to rearrange reality	Acceptance of reality exactly the way it is
Actions spring from desire	Actions flow in harmony with the Tao

CENTERED IN THE SELF	CENTERED IN THE TAO
Desire causes expectations	No expectations
Expectations met, fleeting satisfaction	No fleeting moments
Expectations unmet, disappointment	No disappointment

Feelings

Feelings come and go as desires pull us this way and that	Balanced
Confusion, stress, and sorrow	Peace and serenity
Fleeting satisfaction, moments of happiness	Moments of deep joy
Questions and doubt	Trust
Searching for the way home	Aware we are already home. The Master "arrives without leaving"
Looking for the light	Aware we are always in the light. The Master "sees the light without looking"

Experience of light and darkness

Various shades of darkness in different places	Only light everywhere
Fleeting moments of light that surprise us and are then gone in a flash	Moments of darkness when we let the self take charge for longer than needed

State

At the edge of the circle	At the center of the circle
Asleep in the illusion	Awake in reality

Experience of time

Believes time is real. The future is not yet real. The present is real. The past was real.	Accepts the concept of time but sees it as an illusion of our human experience. In reality, there is no time. (If time existed, it would be eternally present—"now is all there is.") But accepts that this is not what we experience
Visits past with regret or blame	Visits past to learn a little if we can
Visits future with worry or fear	Visits future to plan a little if we can
Often not in the present moment	Mostly in the present moment

CENTERED IN THE SELF	CENTERED IN THE TAO

View of one's talents

See talents as tools to manipulate reality	Discover talents for their own sake, as part of personal opportunity to uniquely express the Tao for the length of a human lifetime
To direct and control	To guide and shape
Self is invested in its work. "Clings" to work to ensure it has the desired result and that the self reaps the rewards	Work is simply an expression of the Tao. "Do your work, then step back" (chapter 9). "If you want to accord with the Tao, just do your job, then let go" (chapter 24)

Purpose of life

Rearrange the world to suit self	Make a positive difference in the world
Deaf to everything except the sound of your own voice	Sing in harmony with the music, which is already there
Satisfy desires within lifetime	Consciously participate in the continuing endless expression of the Tao

I will end with a closing comment on the final row. In the right-hand column it says, "Consciously participate in the continuing endless expression of the Tao." I think it is true to say that we are not consciously aware of having asked for this opportunity to participate. I think we are given this opportunity whether we want it or not. What's more, we can make as much or as little of it as we choose.

Speaking for myself, I know there are times when I fail to see my life as the amazing opportunity that it is. Sometimes the journey feels like going through a dark valley and I can easily forget everything in the right-hand column. When this happens, the *Tao Te Ching* is a wonderful reminder because it shows me the view from the mountaintop. The view reminds me the light is always there.

I believe it doesn't matter who we are or where we are on our journeys; the *Tao Te Ching* will always show us the view from the mountaintop. And, when we are open to it, what we see is indeed an amazing view.

About the Author

FRANCIS PRING-MILL presents ideas in understandable ways to help others gain insights. He has been fascinated by the *Tao Te Ching* since discovering a copy in a secondhand bookstore as a teenager. Written over 2,500 years ago, the *Tao Te Ching* takes us to a mountaintop and shows us amazing views of what it is like to live in harmony with the world around us.

In his first book, *In Harmony with the Tao: A Guided Journey into the Tao Te Ching*, Francis Pring-Mill applies skills developed as a professional facilitator, course developer and instructor, and communicator to offer the reader a guided journey into a densely written ancient spiritual text. In his new book, *There Is No Somewhere Else*, he explores a series of contemporary observations to reveal new insights which also have their roots in the *Tao Te Ching*.

Francis Pring-Mill has a master's degree and a doctorate from the University of Oxford, where he also won a postgraduate scholarship which funded three years of doctoral research. He then held a two-year postdoctoral fellowship at the University of Toronto. In the business world, his roles have included government statistician, software engineer, and director in an IT professional services firm. He has published in the fields of zoology, software engineering, and methodology. His writing is characterized by success at analyzing, simplifying, and presenting ideas to make them easier to understand and apply. In his books, he brings the same skills to a new subject.

If you have enjoyed this book, please consider leaving an online review.

To receive the author's newsletter, please sign up at:
www.francispringmill.com

www.ingramcontent.com/pod-product-compliance
Lightning Source LLC
Chambersburg PA
CBHW060602080526
44585CB00013B/655